CW01647133

CRISPIAN RILEY-SMITH

An Entrepreneur's Odyssey:

My Challenging Journey to Success in the International Art Market

First published by Crispian Riley-Smith 2025

First edition

ISBN: 978-1-9193327-0-3

This book was professionally typeset on Reedsy.
Find out more at reedsy.com

Contents

Preface

I wanted to write a book on my experiences and lessons I have learnt from my career in the Art Market, but I also wanted this book to do so much more. I want it to open the reader's eyes to this opaque business, and to illustrate how much work it took to dedicate myself to this career. I have wanted to write a book for some years; I first started exploring the idea in 2007 and approached a publisher, who wisely instructed me to send me the first chapter. That was clever. I never did. I guess my excuse was I was in the middle of running various art businesses and my second child, Allegra, had just been born. Also, I was not ready or confident enough to do it. My thinking at this time was I write a book on the techniques and scholarship of "Master Drawings"[1], my area of expertise, and one I have spent three decades studying, and continue to work in. This likely would have had a very small readership and was aimed at being educational in this subject area alone. Now 21 years on, my fourth child now four years old, I have written this book. Time focuses things. I am now clearer in knowing what I want from life, and also know that time is short. Despite a very full life, it has shot by and I feel I am looking at a further 15-20 years of an active working career. I know that it will go in the blink of an eye. I hope this book will have wide appeal to all business owners, collectors, dealers and entrepreneurs. In addition provide as a reference to those thinking of

[1] "Master Drawings" is the term used to describe works on paper, rather than paintings, called Master Paintings. That means original drawings, not prints, or sketches on paper, or sometimes vellum, animal skin, or occasionally canvas. This is a very wide field and covers works by European artists around 1400 to 1920s, artists from England, Scotland, France, Germany, Holland, Spain, Italy. The medium can be extremely varied from pencil, to chalks, to pen and ink, watercolour and pastel. Usually these works were the working drawings artists did on a daily basis in preparation for projects or just practice.

setting up a business in the art world. And to those looking for a career in the art world, and maybe give some ideas for those in the art world. I think this will resonate with you.

I also wanted to dispel some myths. There are many books about the art world and the Art Market. In researching this book and reading what other books are out there about the Art Market and collectors, these are some of the most memorable that I have read, but this is by no means an exhaustive list. Frank Herrmann, *Sotheby's: Portrait of an Auction House*, 1981; Georgina Adam, *Darkside of the Boom, The Excesses of the Art Market in the 21st century*, 2018; James Stourton, *Rogues and Scholars: Boom and Bust in the London Art Market,* 2024; Simon de Pury, *The Auctioneer: Adventures in the Art Trade*, 2017; Orlando Whitfield, *All that Glitters: A story of Friendship, Fraud and Fine Art,* 2025; John Richardson, *The Sorcerer's Apprentice: Picasso, Provenance and Douglas Cooper,* 1999; Flavia Ormond, *Stepping Stones: A life of Art and Adventure*, 2023; Lord Hindlip, *An Auctioneer's Lot: Triumphs and Disaster at Christie's*, 2016; Philip Hook, *Rogue's Gallery: A History of Arts and its Dealers*, 2018; Christopher Mason, *The Art of the Steal: Inside the Sotheby's -Christie's Auction House Scandal,* 2004; J.F. Heijbroek, *Frits Lugt 1884-1970,* 2012; Peter Watson and Cecilia Todeschini, *The Medici Conspiracy: The Illicit Journey of Looted Antiquities, from Italy's Tomb Raiders to the World's Great Museums,* 2007. There is some interesting historical information, especially on Sotheby's, by Frank Herrman and the fascinating biography of the incredible dealer/ collector Frits Lugt. I certainly did not want to repeat the same trope or stereotype of the Art Market: wealthy collectors; glamorous parties; crooked dealers. These books and others give a very good description of that. Some people think that working in the art world is a cross between a James Bond movie, without the danger, but plenty of glamour and fast money, and fast art. I am sorry to disappoint you, but that has not been my experience in 37 years.

There are some further books which I have read, unrelated to the Art Market, from which I have drawn inspiration and motivation, and have applied these to my working career. These are some of them, including Steven Pressfield,

The War of Art, 2012, he writes about resistance and all the things that could be stopping us achieve our goals. Atul Gawande, *The Checklist Manifesto*, 2009. The Bible, and in particular the Book of Psalms I find messages of Christian and religious values an essential grounding. Who can argue with forgiveness, kindness, love, thankfulness and contemplation. I often refer to them when I need help and guidance. I am inspired by people like Bear Grylls. I like his honesty, his independence, his attitude to risk, his outdoors approach, his faith. I have read a number of his books, and I particularly like *Mud, Sweat and Fears*, 2012. Ramit Sethi, *I will Teach you to be Rich*, 2009 is a book I find fascinating and entertaining, and I love his podcasts. He has turned a turgid and boring subject, into one of great interest and relevance.

I also love listening to podcasts and particularly like "Social Media Marketing Podcasts" by Michael Stelzner, Social Media Examiner. This helps me get a broad view of the business world, and prevents me from sitting in my art world silo too much.

Working in the Art Market has never been one of glamour and fast money, that has never been my experience. It is hard work and more hard work, and maybe some success along the way. I have not seen many books written about the day to day life of working in the Art Market. I would like this book to be of practical assistance, and to serve as a self-help guide to those of you who are contemplating a career in this market. Many of my contemporaries are looking at retirement, which partly fills me with horror as well as envy! I love the business, but like some love affairs, it is not always reciprocated. As you will see, for me it was often full of anguish, hard work and worries. I do not see this changing immediately, but I do see a different horizon. Yes, I have had fun, yes, I made a bit of money. I always found it strange how collectors did not like a dealer making a profit, and when I asked them what they did they became very quiet and did not like to reveal anything but somehow it was okay for them to ask me everything about me, my stock and where I bought things,and what I was doing. Be under no illusion the money is hard to earn, and there are no guarantees. The profit I made as a dealer was based on my expertise, contacts, my resourcefulness and hard work.

The Art Market is not like the banking or insurance industries where you have many large businesses. There are around 6,500 auction houses[2] worldwide, but these are small businesses. There are roughly 20,000 dealers[3] worldwide, but these are mainly small operations, with a small team, typically a husband and wife or partner. There are only a handful of mega galleries, who employ in their worldwide operations around 400-500 people in their different sites. But these firms make a lot of noise and attract a lot of attention because what they do is unique and often seen as wacky or interesting to a wider public. The pay structure will be very much an upside-down pyramid. The auction houses and dealerships are not like the large behemoths in other industries. Employees come and go because the market cycles are significant, and the margins are small. Those who last are survivors and have worked out how to last in a very cutthroat business.

The Art Market, in financial terms is tiny. The Global Art Market was estimated, in 2024 (referring to 2023 sales figures), to be worth globally $US 65 billion[4]. The global financial markets was $US one quadrillion[5]. Simply the financial markets are 15,000 bigger. It costs a lot of money to sell art works and second hand luxury goods. This is borne by the auction house or dealer, who naturally pass this onto the clients by charging a relatively significant amount in % terms of the transaction. Not surprisingly the fees are typically 30-50% of the sale price for most objects, whether this be at auction or a dealer. This is in the situation of the seller acting as an agent and charging a commission

---

[2] Auction houses typically act as agents in the transaction like an estate agent, but they earn their fees from % commissions from the buyer and seller.

[3] Dealers earn their fee by either buying the works of art as a principal and selling the art work. Their margin is often not known and is made from the purchase price to the selling price. If they act as an agent they usually earn their fee from a commission from the seller, and this could be the artist or owner of the art work.

[4] *The Art Basel & UBS Art Market Report 2024*, by Arts Economics, Dr Clare McAndrew.

[5] Data from LSEG (London Stock Exchange Group).

to the principal. In the financial market this would be unacceptable, and commissions are around 0.5% to 2%, or lower: do the math (as they say in the US). The costs for bringing something for sale to the Art Market are significant, the transaction costs are expensive, and many. And it takes time. An object must be stored, shipped, researched, catalogued, photographed, a buyer found. After sale it has to be shipped again, stored again, insured by the new owner. And this is before any issues occur at any of these points, and problems do occur in their multitude. Also the object may not sell. As a dealer I used to guestimate holding stock from 6 months to 20 years. This is bonkers as far as cash flow is concerned. Can you imagine holding a tomato or an item of clothing for 20 years in the retail market! Selling a stock or share is just a few clicks on a computer and much of this is automated.

On the plus side I do love art and the commerce and the interchange between the two which continues to fascinate and enthrall me on a daily basis. I also love meeting new people, and working in an industry that is constantly changing, but I have a perspective that is valuable and one based on hard work, experience and expertise.

It is interesting to see how in the Art Market some of the financial tools used in the financial world are now being applied, for example fractionalisation, see Chapter .

I also wanted to write to a book so I can make more money for myself and expose my new business to a wider audience. My ambition is to create some charitable foundations and trusts, and I need to make money to do that. I wanted to share all the experience and expertise which I have literally devoted my life to, like some cult. Was it worthwhile, and was it not a waste of my time? I guess I want to have a tangible legacy. I want to find a meaning, and I want to leave a legacy that is both meaningful and positive to the world. There are still so many things I want to do and achieve in my life, and this is just another step on that path.

I also get a lot of messages from graduates, and from those who want to change career, and those coming into the market: how did you start? So this is where

I am directing them, and I hope you will too. But also please do continue to contact me, since I remember only too well how hard I found it to enter into the art world. But I do believe there are now many more opportunities for everyone.

Fig. 1 is a time line of my career, since I have not written this book in a strict chronological order.

Fig. 1 Crispian Riley-Smith Career Timeline	**Wider Activities & World Events**
1970s Selling daffodils Selling eggs	
1985-89 Selling boxer and beach shorts at Univ. Nightclub Holiday job, Sotheby's, Italy Intern, Peggy Guggenheim Museum, Venice	St. Andrews University
1989-1991 Graduate job Sotheby's London Volunteer, British Museum, Dept of Prints & Drgs	Japanese withdrawal from art market August 1990: 1st Gulf War
1991 Phillips, specialist Old Master Drgs Dept.	September 1992: Black Wednesday
1995 Christie's, specialist Old Master Drgs Dept.	Start of the World Wide Web Boom in Contemporary Art Market September 1997: "Sensation" exhibition at Royal Academy, London
1998 Start of 1st business	
2002 Start of 2nd business	March 2003: 2nd Gulf War
2006 Start of 3rd business	September 2008: Global Financial Crisis
2019 Exit from 2nd business	November 2022: Chat GBT released
2023 Sale of 3rd business Start of 4th business	

Acknowledgments

I would like to thank the following people who have helped me on book my writing journey. Sukhi Jutla who I spoke to quite early on in the writing of this book, she gave me one great piece of advice which I have tried to follow. She said to respect the reader. She went on to suggest I go to Reedsy as a tool for writing the book and finding editors. Here I found editors who gave me valuable advice on the structure and direction of my story. The final edits have been done by Emily Riley-Smith and Andrew McKenzie. In put was also received from Cheyenne Westphal. Thank you. All the mistakes or errors are mine, and many of the stories are how I remember them, so there may be factual errors, however I have aimed to keep them as accurate as possible.

In a career spanning 50 years- I am taking 8 as when I first started my first "business"-there are of course many people who have helped me on my journey. I particularly want to thank my wife Emily Riley-Smith who has been unwavering in her support and belief in me. I dedicate this book to her and my four children, Flavia, Allegra, Henry and Violet. They are my motivators.

My late father, Hamish, and my mother, Gita, have been great supporters throughout my life, as well as my brother Damian.

There are many people who have helped me throughout my career and most of them are woven into the text.

I can be reached via email: crispian@artadvisorygroupltd.com or through my website www.artadvisorygroupltd.com I post regularly on LinkedIn and can be followed on www.linkedin.com/in/crispian-riley-smith

Introduction

It was 1983. I was 16 years old and standing in front of a picture which would influence the course of the rest of my life, but I did not know it then.

All I could do was stand transfixed in front of the most beautiful painting I had ever seen. It was of a young man wearing a large red and white doublet beneath a large black jacket with the Maltese cross discreetly showing on the side lapel. It looked like he was wearing a large jacket, but the jacket was incredibly elegant and shimmering. He must have been a similar age to me but down the centuries he looked and behaved like he was 20 years older than me. He stared confidently out in my direction, and was not looking at me, but over my shoulder. Not in a uninterested way, just he was clearly preoccupied with important matters of state. The painting was around 400-500 years old, and to me, it must have been a portrait of an important dignitary or royal person. It was by Titian (c.1488/90-1576), his *Portrait of Ranuccio Farnese as Knight of Malta.*[6]

Titian was one of the foremost Venetian painters in the 16th century, and was noted for his ability to bring "colorito", the colour of pigments to painting. The flip side to this is "disegno" which favoured the art of drawing, and this was mainly practised by the artists from Florence. Clearly it was Titian's masterly use of colour that had me transfixed.

None of this really mattered to me at this point in time, I was just mesmerized. This started me on a journey that has lasted 42 years. I ask you to join me on this odyssey of discovery, learning and beauty, which continues to this day and beyond. At 16 years old I had just started being be interested in art whist

---

[6] *The Genius of Venice 1500-1600*, edited by Jane Martineau and Charles Hope, Royal Academy of Arts, 1983, no. 121, back cover, in the National Gallery of Art, Washington.

attending Eton trying to find my "thing". I knew I had found it there on the steps of the Royal Academy. My mother had taken me to see this exhibition during one of the "exeats".[7] From this point on in my life art would be a daily part of what I did and thought about every day. But before we start on this journey I want to tell you another story.

It was four years later, and I must have been 20 years old. I was on a train hurtling through the Italian countryside with my head out of the window. The sweet smell of pine was rushing through my nostrils. The train was rattling alongside the Arno River in Tuscany, and the smell of the heat and warmth was almost overpowering. It was a stark contrast to the dampness of the Norfolk or the Scottish countryside I was used to. I had just woken up from my international sleeper and it was around 7 or 8 am in the morning, having spent the last 24 hours travelling from London to Florence. This was my first job with Sotheby's[8] and I was very excited about what lay ahead. It felt like all those decisions I had made, first starting after seeing that portrait in the Royal Academy, four years earlier, had led me to where I was now, and I was doing the right thing. I had studied hard at Eton[9] to get some decent grades to get into university so I could read the History of Art. I had spent a lot of time trying to get a "summer" job in Italy and also learn Italian. Finally all those years of hard work had led me to this point. I knew I was in the right tribe and orbit I wanted to be in, but I did not know where it would lead me or really why I wanted to do it. I just knew this is what I wanted to do.

---

[7] Exeats were mini breaks from school, and lasted either a day or a weekend.

[8] In 1986 Sotheby's auction house had an office and saleroom in Florence, the latter was in the stunning Palazzo Capponi.

[9] Eton College, Windsor, I studied there from 1981 till 1985. The Art History department and Art Schools were my main focus of enjoyment and studies.

1

Chapter 1: Early Businesses, from Daffodils to a Nightclub

Just start the business.

As an entrepreneur I do spend a lot of time thinking and planning. But the wonderful thing as a child and young adult, I just started the businesses. I did not think about the consequences. The ramifications of not setting a business up correctly and thinking all of this through from entry to exit will have significant repercussions later down the line. Like the "butterfly effect", the analogy of butterfly wings on a pond. My first few businesses were selling things, like eggs, daffodils, boxer and beach shorts and a nightclub. Thankfully these did not require any planning.

I loved the idea of selling something, and since I was living in the countryside as a child the two things that easily came to my hands were daffodils and eggs. These were easy enough to sell and came with it the instant gratification of collecting the money from the "honesty" box. As an adult this is something I started to do with my children, and they have all enjoyed it, and possibly I am a bit too enthusiastic on this journey with them. It is the instant result which I loved, like some drug. You did something, and you saw the immediate result. Just so exciting and invigorating. A real high.

When I was at St Andrews University [10] in 1987 I had the idea of starting a nightclub from my brother, Damian,[11] who had set up a nightclub in Cambridge University, a few years earlier. When I went to St Andrews the only nightclub as such in the town was a student disco on a Friday night. So, I joined up with a friend, Johnny Churchill[12]. We joined forces and decided to approach the hotels which had the space and set up for a dance floor and bar. Johnny was good at music and had great social contacts. I was good at marketing, and making things happen and had good social contacts too, a bit more artsy. So we combined forces and walked around to several of the hotels and asked them if they were interested in their premises being filled with 100-200 students drinking at their bars on a Thursday night, during the university term time. St Andrews in the winter months can be quiet. We were confident we could fill the bars-such is the confidence of youth! But we were right. Before long the St Andrews Golf Hotel[13] said we could use their function room at the back, which had a separate entrance off the Score's at the back, through a rather grim car park (Fig 2.4). Crucially it contained a bar and dance floor on the ground floor, and a snug room and bar on the lower ground floor for those who just wanted to drink, smoke -yes, in those days it was legal to smoke indoors- and chat. So, for the opening term I teamed up with some friends and created a committee. I created a committee since I thought it would be helpful to get other friends, and friends of friends, to spread the word across the university and years. Which it did. I ordered some credit cards (Fig. 2.3) which was the members pass, bought some records, found a DJ, and rented the music deck belonging to the university. We needed a DJ to work the sound system and mix the tracks one after another. This was a skilled job and I never gave it a try. Johnny was good and often took to the decks if our DJ did not

---

[10] I went to St Andrews University in 1985 to read "Art History", the degree is an M.A. rather than a B.A., and is achieved after four years of studies.

[11] Damian Riley-Smith owns a number of publishing and events businesses, through his company Paragraph Publishing.

[12] John Churchill is working for a financial firm in the US.

[13] St Andrews Golf Hotel is now the Hotel du Vin, on the Scores.

turn up. Which happened quite regularly. The credit cards were incredibly popular and sold like hot cakes. These cards were not credit cards as such, but were an exclusive card, like a golden ticket, which gave the holders a sense of belonging to something exclusive.

After the first few Thursday evenings we found that the taxis would be queuing up outside the exit, in the car park at 12:45 am, knowing that the doors would be spilling out students wanting to go back to their rooms at 1:00 am, when the club closed. This was an endorsement of the success of Katie's and that it had arrived as an event in the calendar of student life. I found that incredibly satisfying. Also making some money made life as a student better.

Fig. 2.1 Marketing material for Katie's

Fig. 2.2 Alcohol was a big pull for students

Fig. 2.3
The "Katie's" membership card, styled as a credit card carried cudos

Fig. 2.4 Author outside "Katie's" with speakers from the students union

This ran successfully for two years, and we sold it on to another student in the year below us.

I guess it taught me we could influence our market very easily since they were students, and we knew where they "hung out" and how to reach them: which was the library, the student's union, the diners, and by leaving these marketing flyers on the window screens of cars. St. Andrews is a small town and this was way before the internet or any form of mobile phone. It was face to face or word of mouth.

Our means of communication was so effective we could run a "campaign" on the Tuesday and know we could reach our audience for the Thursday night, see some of the original marketing material (Fig 2.1 and Fig. 2.2).

Crucially it was fun, and I often think back to that time, and how much fun we had. At times I wish I could infuse that sense of fun in what I do now. I see no reason why work can not be fun and an adventure, rather than a duty or some chore. But that is sometimes easier said that done. I admire people like Richard Branson for making work fun.

2

Chapter 2: Why a career in the Art World?

This is a question that every Art History Graduate, Artist, Auctioneer, and Gallerist[14] will have asked themselves, and I am sure will continue to ask themselves when it is tough, and are struggling to find a job, or earn money from their skills. This is where we start to get into the serious questions of how to make money in the Art Market. Why do you want a career in the Art Market? Do you think you can make money easily? Do you like the art? Is this a real job?

I have always been drawn towards art. It was always my thing. Something that I connected to and was good at. It was at Eton that I was able to really explore and start to fully dive into this art interest in the Art Schools. I won the senior sculpture prize, and still have the art work in my office. I went to art classes and started drawing and sculpting (see Fig. 3.1 and Fig. 3.2) and took on Art as an extra course at O'Level [15] and A'Level. The art schools at Eton were extremely well resourced, and there was encouragement for anything

---

[14] Gallerist is someone who works in a gallery, and it is typically front of house, the person the public first meets. But also the most common jobs they have are doing odd jobs. I worked as a gallerist in Richard Demarco's gallery in Edinburgh during one holiday in the 1980s. He was a significant figure in the cultural landscape in Edinburgh.

[15] O'Level (literally Ordinary Level) was the precurser to GCSEs and stopped in 1987/8.

creative from my house master. He was Raef Payne, [16] and he was incredibly supportive and enthusiastic for the creative arts. He was particularly keen on directing plays, and understood how important an outlet this could be. My good friend John Martin[17] was a keen and skilled draftsman and painter, and we were in the same house and year and we have both been on this path since we were school boys. I spent most of my free time in the art schools, which were located at the other end of the school campus, and took me away from the activities of the house. It was definitely somewhere I could escape to.

[16] Raef Payne, known by his initials R.J.G.P. was my house master at Eton until he left the house in 1983.

[17] John Martin has his own gallery in London and Suffolk.

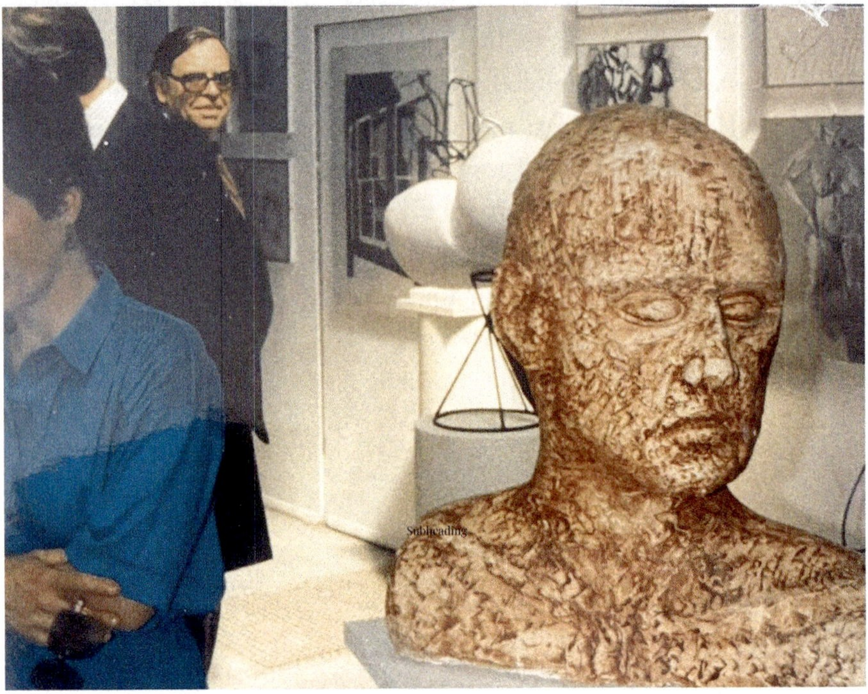

Fig. 3.1 "Head" sculpture by the author in the Art Schools at Eton, author's father in background

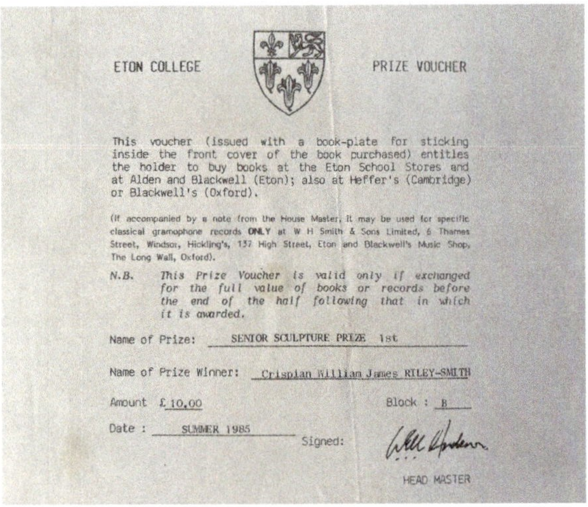

ETON COLLEGE PRIZE VOUCHER

This voucher (issued with a book-plate for sticking inside the front cover of the book purchased) entitles the holder to buy books at the Eton School Stores and at Alden and Blackwell (Eton); also at Heffer's (Cambridge) or Blackwell's (Oxford).

(If accompanied by a note from the House Master, it may be used for specific classical gramophone records **ONLY** at W H Smith & Sons Limited, 6 Thames Street, Windsor, Hickling's, 137 High Street, Eton and Blackwell's Music Shop, The Long Wall, Oxford).

N.B. *This Prize Voucher is valid only if exchanged for the full value of books or records before the end of the half following that in which it is awarded.*

Name of Prize: SENIOR SCULPTURE PRIZE 1st

Name of Prize Winner: Crispian William James RILEY-SMITH

Amount £10.00 Block : B

Date : SUMMER 1985 Signed:

HEAD MASTER

Fig. 3.2 Author's prize of Senior Sculpture prize, never used, for the above sculpture

I did enjoy looking and learning about objects, whether it be a 1920s Art Deco item of jewellery or a Lucio Fontana rip painting[18] or a Francis Bacon (1909-1992) triptych painting,[19] and was wondering why was something worth a certain value. At one time I was thinking of buying a Francis Bacon rug that came up at auction, when I was at Sotheby's. It sold for a modest amount,[20] which taught me an early lesson, which is that the market wants the obvious works done by great artists. It does not want the "Black Swan", since this is not commercially attractive. The market wants to buy the triptych of screaming popes by Francis Bacon. This is an incredibly subjective thing, and one that is constantly fascinating to me. The market wants the typical examples. If you buy an Andy Warhol you want something that is familiar, such as his series of portraits, such as Marilyn Monroe, or an image of Campbell's soup tins.

So why did I dedicate my life to art?

Art takes you to other places. When I look at a painting that I know well or have known for many years, memories come flooding back, like listening to music from a particular time in my life. For example if I am listening to music, such as "Good Vibrations" by the Beach Boys it brings me back to memories of parties as a teenager. Or "Bohemian Rhapsody" by Queen: I can literally visualise the moment listening to this with friends at university. Art, like music, brings back memories and moments in time. It also takes me to different places in my mind. Going into a museum, like The National Gallery in London, is almost a religious experience. Many of the paintings

---

[18] Lucio Fontana (1898-1968), Argentine-Italian painter, who is typically known for his canvases which have a blank neutral colour, like white or blue, and have a careful rip down the centre.

[19] Francis Bacon was known for his triptych paintings of screaming popes. The triptych was a three painting format which was something he repeated again and again.

[20] Sotheby's London, 22 February, 1990, lot 308, "Hand made wool rug", sold for £4,800 hammer. Hammer is the amount the auctioneer's hammer drops down on. This is before auctioneer's premium and any additional taxes or costs.

and altarpieces were once in churches. The "Burlington House Cartoon"[21], by Leonardo da Vinci, the only drawing owned by the National Gallery, if you exclude the pastels, is in its own side chapel behind the "The Virgin of the Rocks" [22] by the same artist. Going round the galleries is like seeing old friends, but they do not age, they remain the same. They spark images of past experiences and moments in my life, like slides passing through my head, and bringing back those memories in my life. "Portrait of Susanna Lunden (?)"[23] by Rubens reminds me of a cover of book I studied as a student. The unfinished painting "The Manchester Madonna"[24], by Michelangelo of another book cover. The exquisite Albrecht Dürer painting, which is painted on both sides by the artist and has the depiction of "St. Jerome" [25] on one side, and a bizarre astrological sign on the other, neatly enclosed in a perspex box. It is extraordinary to think this painting was for years hanging at Raveningham Hall[26] in Norfolk. To continue the religious trajectory, churches in Italy and the UK had chapels which were funded by the wealthy, and dedicated to their loved ones and their family. Now galleries in the UK receive financial gifts to the memory of loved ones, such as The Julia Rausing Trust[27]. Indeed I used to work with Julia at Christie's and she was a lovely person. In the museums there are even card readers to make your donation easy, like in the Church of England foyers.

So why do I want to understand value in art? I want to understand why a book

---

[21] *The Virgin and Child with Saint Anne and the Infant Saint John the Baptist*, NG6337

[22] NG1093

[23] NG852

[24] NG809

[25] NG6563

[26] Raveningham Hall is a Grade II listed Hall that the Bacon family have lived in since 1735.

[27] The Julia Rausing Trust was created by Sir Hans Rausing to realise the philanthropy of Sir Hans Rausing and honour the memory of Julia. It has recently donated £150 million to the National Gallery for the creation of a new gallery. This is on top of £4 million already given in 2018. Julia sadly died of cancer in 2024.

or a drawing is worth a value and why these changes occur. Throughout my career in the market, I have seen prices change, and the market prices go up and down. The assumed trajectory is that prices always go up is just simply not the case. What do I get from it? I earn money from my knowledge, expertise and experience. I cover this more in Chapter 9, Art as an Investment.

Destiny

One question I have reflected on over the years is how much your family heritage affects how you do things, and your attitude to your work and ambition. I know it has affected mine. I come from a family that built businesses. My father was very keen on this and encouraged me and my brother to set up our own business from an early age. I guess it was because my father came from a family of brewers, John Smith's from Tadcaster[28], and he felt an important responsibility to create businesses and wealth for the next generation. I am not sure this was always the right thing, but it came from a place of genuine belief. By this I mean that wealth can and is created by being an employee in a company. But this is not the path I am on now. Yes it was when I was working as an employee in an auction house, and I left this full time employment blanket in 1998. Yes I can change this narrative, and I have. But it is a strong path. I think it is like how some families are doctors or in the army. Our family are artists, collectors, and business creators[29]. That is the narrative that I chose but also I wanted to create businesses that served a purpose and were a force for good or change. But I want more than that. I want to think about my legacy. Why create a business? Because I want to leave something positive behind. When creating a business you leave a part of yourself in it. It is personal. You created it, had the idea, and put everything

[28] The last of the family interest in John Smith's was sold by my grandfather, Douglas Riley-Smith (1914-1981), in 1970.

[29] My great grandmother Ivie Hertslet (1883-1977) was at Lambeth Art School with Glyn Philpot and Eric Kennington; her daughter Mrs Douglas Riley-Smith (1920-1990) was a collector. My relations on my father's side were business owners in the brewing industry and minting industries in Leeds and Birmingham.

into it. I think this was inspired by my father and his attitude to business, but I also wanted to add my belief and character to these businesses.

Your destiny.

I do not believe people who say "oh I just happened to walk into this job" or "that business fell into my lap". You need a vision, you need a plan, you need an idea. This plan will change, and that is fine since life changes, and plans change. Aim for Mars and you will reach the moon. But if you do not know where you want to go how can you say yes or no to what is offered to you on that journey or recognise the opportunities?

I had an idea and a plan with my Art dealing business[30], but various things came along to which I did not react to in time and change. Also I did not review this plan regularly enough. My excuse was I was running *Master Drawings London*[31] and *Master Drawings New York*[32] and my dealing business *Crispian Riley-Smith Fine Arts Ltd*, all from North Yorkshire. Plus, at the time, I had three children. I was also doing four art fairs[33] a year. They were "pop up" exhibitions in different locations and varied from London[34], New York[35],

[30] Dealing is when you buy an object and sell it, and you act as principal and take the risk and the gain.

[31] The first event was in 2001, but the idea and plans had started in 2000, after my first exhibitions on Bond Street had been in 1999 and 2000.

[32] The first event was in 2006, but I had started to plan this in 2005 after my first commercial exhibition in a gallery in New York.

[33] Art fairs tend to last from 5 days to 7 days depending on the location. But with the set up and take down can usually mean 10 days devoted to each location.

[34] Master Drawings London, from 2002-16; and numerous iterations of the Print Fair at the Royal Academy; and the Watercolour and Drawings Fairs at the Royal Geographical Society.

[35] The New York International Antiquarian Fine Art Fair, 2001; The International Fine Art Fair, 2002-4; Shepherd Derom Galleries with Margot Gordon, 2005; Master Drawings New York from 2006-16.

Florence,[36] Amsterdam[37], TEFAF Maastricht[38], Paris[39], and pop up shows in Skipton, Harrogate, at country houses and historical locations, such as Scampston Hall[40] and Skipton Castle[41] in North Yorkshire. I was so busy I could not see the wood from the trees. I could not see the economic tsunami coming my way. The supply in Master Drawings had been drying up for years, the collectors were getting increasingly picky, and only wanting to fill gaps in their collection, and there were not enough new buyers coming into the market hoovering up drawings. I did not diversify my business soon enough. I simply did not invest in a broader product base soon enough. By the time I realised this I felt I had had enough of dealing and art fairs and wanted a complete change. This happened for several reasons, and without beating myself up about it and looking at it objectively I would say it was because I did not have a team of advisers or trusted people who knew enough about my business or were working for me. Those who were close to me, were just happy for the ride. The treadmill of doing four art fairs a year had became a chore, and extremely stressful. I was running two of these fairs, as well as exhibiting in them. One functioning in London, the other in New York. I was doing all of this from North Yorkshire, and later Norfolk.

I knew I had to make a significant change to my working career, and I still wanted to work in the Art Market, which I knew well and was good at.

---

[36] Cartanica, 3rd Master Drawings and Prints Fair, Palazzo Corsini, Florence, 12 October-14 October 2001.

[37] Crispian Riley-Smith at Hein A.M. Klaver Kunsthandel, Amsterdam, 4 November till 9 November 2000.

[38] I showed in TEFAF Maastricht in 2011 in the showcase. This is the premier art fair for traditional and contemporary art in Holland.

[39] Chez William Vonthron, 40, rue de Verneuil, Paris, Cercle Beaux-Arts Rive Gauche, 20 Mars au 26 Mars 2007.

[40] Scampston Hall and walled Garden is located near Malton, North Yorkshire.

[41] Skipton Castle is a medieval Castle in the market town of Skipton, on the edge of the Yorkshire Dales, near to where I used to live.

Now making those rebrands and new business decisions is hard and scary. But I felt I had to do it. If I wanted to achieve the things I wanted to achieve I needed a radical re-think. This was very challenging and frightening and full of concerns. But I felt compelled to do it. I had to do it for myself, I had to dig deep and risk it all again. Start a new business. Start a new life. No guarantees.

My original idea

Part of my initial idea and plan was to become an expert, and do this through the auction houses in London, and the idea was to sell Old Masters drawings. I was going to provide a product which people wanted and collected. I knew that there were plenty of private collectors and institutions interested and actively buying.

By about 2019 I realised I had to pivot and stop dealing and the art fairs to create a new business. For many years I had done valuations for clients, including diverse collections, and I was always able to bring in a team for these jobs. I was also used to selling pictures and objects for clients. I had helped clients buy collections. This was surely Art Advisory?

However I also realised I needed to create a new company and *Crispian Riley-Smith Fine Arts Ltd* would forever be linked in most people's minds as a specialist in Old Master Drawings. This was a very small part of the Art Market pie, and would be commercially restrictive.

To create a business that really had the chance of growing into something much bigger than myself I needed to have a re-think, and use my skills from the past 30 years. Plus bring in a team. But in the mean time I had also to sell *Master Drawings New York*, and complete the 2023 iteration of this event, which was like a black hole in consuming time and energy and thinking, and start a new business. I was trying to get the *Master Drawings New York* event under way and working with the team in the US and all the exhibitors and partners[42]. I had had a bruising time, like many businesses during Covid from 2020-22, and I had to take out Covid loans, and repay them, and keep all the exhibitors and interested parties on board. I had felt for a few years that I needed to sell this business and have it run from New York, rather than North Yorkshire, or Norfolk where I was now living.

A new business:

I spent about four to six months working with Ed Wood[43] to create a new business from scratch. He was excellent at making me think out of my comfort zone and thinking big. We would meet every few weeks, over Zoom of course, and I would be set tasks. I then worked with a lawyer, and art collector, who I had known for a number of years, Wayne Rapozo,[44]. I was also working with my wife Emily[45], who is trained as a lawyer, thinking about these contracts and agreements for buyers, sellers, valuations, specialists and non disclosure agreements. This was hard work and at the time I was selling another business *Master Drawings New York*. Also I was getting married, which had been delayed due to Covid.

I had been running *Master Drawings New York* with Margot Gordon[46], but she had retired a few years earlier and Covid did not help. However, remarkably we had kept running throughout Covid with a part on-line and part physical version. A lot of businesses in the exhibition space had had to go into

---

[42] Typically for the event in New York there were 16-22 exhibitors, and about 4-6 Museum and Institutional partners and other commercial partners.

[43] Ed Wood is my business advisor and mentor, and also an author.

[44] Wayne James Rapozo is a partner in Corporate Finance firm in London, and a collector of drawings.

[45] Emily Riley-Smith was a partner at a law firm in Chicago, and now works as an Interior Designer and Senior Business Advisor to AAG.

[46] Margot Gordon was a dealer in New York in Master Drawings, and we shared an exhibition space in the Upper East side, at Shepherd-Derom, then Shepherd W & K Galleries, on 79th Street.

hibernation.

I am incredibly proud of what I had achieved with the team, but it was time to move on and that was not easy. I sold the business to Christopher Bishop[47], and it continues to flourish under his leadership and his team, and am thrilled with this outcome. Sadly the same was not true for *Master Drawings London*[48], then *London Art Week*, but I had exited from that in 2019.

Now the problems I had experienced in these businesses had been exasperated because I never had a clear structure or vision or exit plan when the businesses were set up. Like most entrepreneurs, I just wanted to set up the business. I had set up these two art fairs/ art walks[49] to support my main dealing business. I did not expect them to grow into some massive administrative machine which took up my time, effort, energy and money and be some administrator for other art dealers, most of whom were happy to jump on the successes of it.

Inspiration & Influences

I find it really helpful to find ideas and inspiration from my heroes. I often turn to books, and now increasingly podcasts. I love reading. I am also an obsessive visitor to museums, galleries, churches, ruins of any kind, heritage sites and country houses. I am a visual consumer. I love looking at houses and objects and pictures. I also love listening to music.

As a teenager, and as an adult, I was never inspired by stars on the football pitch or cricket or golf, I just was not interested. It was like looking at someone

[47] Christopher Bishop owns Christopher Bishop Fine Art, and is a drawings dealer based in New York, on the upper East side of Manhattan.

[48] *Master Drawings London* was started in 2001 and progressed to *Master Drawings and Sculpture Week* in 2013 and then *London Art Week* in 2016.

[49] Art Fairs are usually associated with a single location in a rented space or a specially built structure. Art walks are located in a gallery space, and other similar galleries are open at the same time, and in walking distance.

who was speaking a different language. For me artists are my heroes. Artists I understood. I loved reading about their lives, their struggles, and in some way I identified with them. I loved reading and learning about their stories and exertions, such as the French draftsman and engraver Rodolphe Bresdin (1822-1885), who was so poor he lived in a pigsty. Or Jacone, who was supposed to be so messy that he ate off his drawings, instead of off a plate[50]. Indeed his drawings are characterised by their messy condition. Luca Giordano, who was called "Fa Presto"[51] because he was so quick at drawing. Or reading the biographies about Picasso by Jonathan Richardson[52] or David Hockney by Christopher Sykes.[53]

I like to see and understand the creative thought process and how an artist reached a composition or conclusion. I think this is why I was attracted to drawings, because you can literally see the creative process in front of you. Paintings are a labour of effort and energy, often over many years. It is well known that artists such as Michelangelo, Picasso and Leonardo would leave paintings or sculptures in their studios for years and come back to them. Therefore paintings often hide the creative process, and appear static to me, after I have studied drawings.

I did think of being an artist when I was at Eton, but I was put off by the fact

---

50 Jacope Di Giovanni Di Francesco (d.1553); Giorgio Vasari, who met the artist, wrote that Jacone was part of a "Hippy" society and went on to describe his life style: "under the pretence of living the philosophic life, lived like pigs and cattle, never washing hands or face or head or beard, never cleaning their houses or making their beds, except once every two months ... and this they thought the best life in the world", G. Vasari, *Le vite de'piu ecclenti pittori, scultori ed architettpri*, ed. Florence, 1878-8.p.452, quoted from Christie's New York, Old Master Drawing, 30 January 1997, lot 11.

51 Luca Giordano, called Fa Presto (1634-1705), his technique of drawing was described by a contemporary biographer, B. De Dominici, *Vite de'Pittori, Scultori ed Architetti Napoletani*, Naples, 1742-5, pp. 396-7.

52 *A Life of Picasso, Volume I, 1881-1906*, 1991; *Volume II: 1907-1917*, 1996; *Volume III, 1917-1932*, 2009; *Volume IV, 1933-1943*, 2022; all by Jonathan Richardson.

53 *Hockney: The Biography, Volume I & Volume II*, 2011 and 2014, by Christopher Simon Sykes.

that very few artists earned their living from their skill. Indeed I remember at the time, circa 1985, someone said to me, only three artists earn their living through their art: Francis Bacon, Henry Moore (1898-1986) and Elizabeth Frink (1930-1993). If the truth be told I did not have the drive or determination to follow this field. Today there are around 50,000 people in the UK earning a living through their creative ability of crafts, sculptures, painting, print making, illustrating. Being an entrepreneur, to me is very creative, I put my heart and soul into my work. I can be creative, and am creating companies, and work for me and for the people I work with. Indeed this book is a creative act. Also owning your own business is a lonely experience, and I imagine being an artist, in a studio by yourself is also lonely. Many of the struggles they experience are also felt by an entrepreneur. They need to rely on their creativity and ingenuity. Think of Salvator Dalì (1904-1989). Think of Richard Branson. Think of Elon Musk, the list goes on. They are show offs for good reason. We might laugh at them, but who has the last laugh?

Since I have visited so many museums I have wondered why should we care about museums and their heritage? The worldwide cultural landscape is going through a significant re-think of how we should interact with these spaces. I think museums are almost like a church, where we can contemplate and think and be inspired. Why is art so important for a region or a nation? I believe that art stimulates memory and emotions like smells do, like the smell of freshly cut grass reminds me of tennis courts and spring and the future summer to come. Art takes us away from reality and allows us to dream. Why do the Greeks get so agitated about the Elgin Marbles? Why do tribes want their heritage back? All of this is quite understandable because there is so much emotion tied up in art and objects, and our identity.

I have also been inspired by historical figures. Especially Winston Churchill. I guess being obsessed by history he was a natural choice. One fascinating fact to me was he used to cry frequently, and often in public. The Windsors had a cruel nick name for him: they used to call him "cry baby". Well how did that work out for them? How did history treat them and Churchill? Now I also identified with this because I cry at the drop of a hat – my children are forever embarrassed about that! I used to feel very embarrassed about that until I read this. Not any more.

I have been inspired by teachers, such as by Mr Coleridge,[54] who taught me History and Geography, and who believed in me when I was struggling at school, and I did well in the subjects he taught me. Which not surprisingly was history. Another source of inspiration for me was my sculpture teacher at Eton, Bob Catchpole[55].

Where do business ideas come from?

I am always amazed at where my business ideas come from and how they develop. I find there are a few things I need to have or be mindful of. I need to be relaxing, going for a walk, at the gym or reading a book. This is where the magic starts. I don't necessarily remember exactly where the ideas germinate, but my mind needs to be in neutral. I cannot be receptive if I am working at full speed getting a job done. This is "do the job" mode and my mind is too focused on finishing the project.

I remember why I started *Master Drawings London:* it was out of frustration. I was fed up of trying to join an art fair in Paris, the *Salon du Dessin*[56]. I was improving my spoken French and written French by taking night classes, and every year writing to the Salon committee. Asking if I could be invited to exhibit. I think after two or three years of rejections I decided to set up a new art fair in London. The formula for *Master Drawings London* was clearly a success. But it required a huge amount of time and energy which took a lot

[54] Mr Coleridge was a teacher at my prep school, Beeston Hall School, in North Norfolk. He believed in me when I failed my first entrance exams to Eton.

[55] Bob Catchpole was a teacher of Sculpture at the Art Schools at Eton for almost 30 years.

[56] *Salon du Dessin* is the premier fair for dealers to exhibit and sell Master Drawings, and was started in 1991, in Paris.

away from my main business. I also did not want to rely on a Parisian art fair. I wanted to build up my own client base, and build something I could do every year and be guaranteed to be a part of.

Dreams and ambitions

I think dreams and ambitions are really important, and to think big is important to do and is exciting. No project, no business starts unless a person has an idea. No bridge, no building, is started unless someone says I want to do that. To me this is such a simple, but mind-blowing concept. But along this journey you will need help from many people, and you will need to be good at working or encouraging other people to see your vision and why they should be involved. My philosophy and style is not one of forcing people or being aggressive or bullying. I would rather bring people along with me. But I have realised I need to be tough at times, and whilst this is not my natural mode, I can and am when required. This is because the end goal requires it.

3

Chapter 3: Forming my vision and plan for the future

It is important to have an end goal. Why are you spending all this time and effort and energy on something? What is your motivation? What is your plan? There are many things that motivate us as an individual and this will change over time depending on your stage in life. I think it is important to carefully think what motivates you. You need to be honest with yourself. Why do you want to work in this field? You need to carefully answer this question and be honest with yourself. Since the commitment it requires is significant.

Now I am in a rush to get things done. I acknowledge my own mortality is now not far. If I am lucky another 30 years, probably another 15-20 years of an active working life. I see my career with the art world continuing, but I also see more time being spent creating charities and trusts and doing some public work. Quite what this looks like I do not know, but I am not interested in doing front line elected politics, I tried this and it is brutal[57]. When I was younger I would power through the work deadlines, and travel a lot for work. However by doing exercise and a mindset of working I am confident I will continue to have an active and healthy life. I do find it extraordinary how one focus of

[57] I stood as a District Councillor in 2019, 2023 and County Councillor in 2021, in North Norfolk.

my British colleagues and friends is retiring. It is not as if my friends and colleagues have been working in the front line services, such as the Army, or Police or the Fire Service. I want to continue to work well into my 70s and may be 80s. Now I do find this "I want to work" mindset much more prevalent in Americans, and I am not just saying this because I am married to an American. I came across this frequently through my 18 years of doing art fairs there, and speaking to them. I do not hear Americans talking about retirement in the same way we "Brits" talk about it. Many Americans are actively working well into their 80s. Look at the current and past Presidents in America. I think it is important to keep your mind active and stimulated. I find it incredibly depressing to hear friends talking about retirement, but I guess that is just me and how I feel about it.

It is said that we humans as a species have a number of motivators underlying all our behaviour, and one needs to understand what these are in yourself and in others. These are some of the main ones: money, sex, family status, position within society. It is important to understand what your motivation is. One business advisor I know said it was just one, "what is in it for me"? I am not so cynical, and I think it is more nuanced. As a young adult, and during a lot of my adult life, I was never really that motivated by money. I was motivated by a desire to follow what interested me and what I found challenging. Of course I needed to pay my way, but I never built up a fighting fund. Now I realise this was not a great strategic choice and have since changed my view.

There were various career avenues I could have gone down, which could have been more financially lucrative, if that was my motivator. For example if I decided to stay at Sotheby's and get a gemmological qualification[58] this would have guaranteed me a career in this part of the Art Market which is very stable, and profitable. When I was working at this auction house I had various choices. Do I focus on Contemporary & Modern Art? This had been one of my areas of interest at university. Francis Bacon was a favourite artist

[58] FGA, Fellowship of Gem-A.

of mine and I had done my dissertation on him at university, for my Masters degree. He was someone I felt very keen on, and connected to. Also the whole "London School" of artists had interested me. But now I was in the Art Market I was drawn to other areas such as Old Masters and wanted to work in this department- but there was no space. My interest in Old Masters had grown since my studies at St. Andrews, and had developed during the time I worked at Sotheby's in Florence and the two months I had spent in Venice working at the Peggy Guggenheim museum. I had visited many museums and churches in both cities, and this was a subject that I was deeply interested in, and wanted to learn more about. At the time I felt this modern field was just vacuous and focused on the money. I wanted to be challenged. I have subsequently changed my view and realise this was just my view, and how I felt at the time, and that it is much more complicated and nuanced.

Whilst working at Sotheby's London as a graduate trainee, my eyes had been opened to other areas in the Art Market. I had been working in the jewellery department and was encouraged to work here and get the gemmology certifications. But this did not interest me that much, and I did not want to devote my career to this field, which only partially interested me. Other departments were suggested but I said no. So, I was let go. Another major turning point. Did I think about this carefully enough? Another opportunity would have been to stay at Phillips, and not move to Christie's, since I was being offered the opportunity to stay with Phillips. Instead I moved to Christie's. This did make for some significant choices which were not helpful to me economically. I now realise that I need money to do the things that I want to do. What will motivate you to get up in the morning day after day? When things are not looking good what pushes you on? We all have low days, and as a business owner this can seem relentless. No money coming in, and bills to pay the whole time. It can get very overwhelming. I have been there many times, and it has taken a toll on my health and wellbeing. I do not want to dwell on this since I am a believer in positive thinking and solving problems, and have put many of these demons to rest.

It is important to surround yourself with people who believe in you; not "yes" people; but people who are on your team and not trying to undermine you, people who support you and your vision- you will need it, I can guarantee that.

Any business needs to make money and to make money your business must supply either one of two things. A service and or a product. Either or both must be relevant. There must be a need for it. If your product becomes out of fashion or there is no longer a need then the business stops. Who needs video tapes anymore? Where are *Blockbusters*? Where are *Virgin Records*? *Virgin Records* were smart enough to re-invent themselves and broaden their offer and risk. Think of *Yellow Pages*, now *Yell.com*, which is completely transformed from their previous iteration.

About three years ago I started a new art advisory business, *Art Advisory Group* (Fig .4.1). Advisory work was always something I had done but as a dealer, but as *Crispian Riley-Smith Fine Arts* I felt that I would not be able to grow into a significant business since I would already be thought of as a dealer in Master Drawings. I needed to punch above my weight and create a business that was bigger than me or my persona. Also if I created a business that grew big enough I could make more money.

Fig. 4.1 The author speaking at The Art Business Conference at the launch of AAG in 2023

Fig. 4.2 Meeting with AAG specialists and business services at The Estorick Collection, London

This was not an easy decision because I already had a dealing business, which I had spent 25 years on, and building up, and had just re-branded as an art advisor, under my trading name of *Crispian Riley-Smith Fine Arts Ltd.* It felt like I was having to start all over again. And in some ways, I was. But now I had over three decades of experience and had seen all sides of the business in the art world from the primary market to art fairs, to dealing to museums, to collectors.

The Art Market is full of fascinating persona and people, who come in and out over time. Some are passing through, onto other careers, after they have given the art world a try. Some stay the course. But now I wanted to create a long-lasting business that would be around long after I had gone.

What is the business model?

By this I mean how and when does the money come in?

In my experience this is how it works if you are a dealer or a gallery. Not if you are an agent or an auction house. This is an important distinction, and I think it is missed by many people. Indeed many people complain how crazy it is for a gallery to charge 50-70% to the artist. I will explain why. I am not saying this is what must happen, I am just explaining how it works on the economics. An auction house usually charges clients between 30-40%[59] in fees, before taxes and other costs. This is because the transaction costs are significant. In monetary terms these are small figures, therefore the percentages need to be high, and have only been going in this direction since the 1970s, when buyer's premiums were first introduced.[60]

59 An auction houses typically charges the seller between 10-15% and the buyer between 20-25%.

60 Buyer's premium was first introduced on 4 September 1975 at a Sotheby's silver sale, and was initially 10%, and VAT was not charged at the time, this was introduced later. Previously only the sellers paid the fees.

This is the buying process I used to go through when I was actively looking to buy stock on a daily basis as a dealer. First I needed to find the object. This was not a problem since each day there are literally dozens of auctions happening. I used to spend 2-3 hours a day trawling through websites looking for lots that interested me[61]. This was great before everyone was doing it and I could, and did, make significant finds. But before I go into this let me explain how it worked before the mass publication of e-catalogues or on-line bidding. When I started dealing in 1998 most catalogues were printed. This meant I would trawl through the Antiques Trade Gazette[62] and the La Gazette Drouot[63]. By this I mean I would literally go over every page and look for any description to do with drawings and trace down the auction house. For those in France I would have to send off a cheque in the post and then wait for the catalogue to arrive. I had some amazing opportunities and tried many times to bid on drawings in Paris or rural France. It was tough since the ground in France was extremely well covered and the trade did not miss a thing. There was one particular drawing, by Denys Calvaert[64] (Fig.5.1. and Fig.5.2), an artist I particularly liked, which I saw coming up for a sale in France. The auction was in Orléans. I decided to do some research and went to the libraries and found it was listed in an important collection of Saint-Morys[65], a provenance which the auctioneers had already identified. The drawing looked stunning from the catalogue. I thought I must buy it. So I asked another dealer if they wanted to come in half-shares with me, and they did. I had to see it since in those days digital images were not going to be sent and they probably did not have the means. Anyway I was determined to come back with the drawing and

[61] There are plenty of websites making finding these objects simple, now there is the-saleroom.com covering most of the UK auction houses, except the bigger auction houses are not on this; there is Interencheres.com covering most of France; and Invaluable.com

[62] A weekly trade magazine read by most dealers in the UK, otherwise known as the ATG.

[63] This is the French equivalent to the ATG

[64] Denys Calvaert (1540-1619), was a Flemish artist who spent most of his career in Italy.

[65] The collector Charles Paul Jean-Baptiste de Bourgevin Vialart de Saint-Morys (1743-1795) had an important collection of drawings, and I found the drawing listed in his collection. Once this sort of information is found it opens up more doors on the drawings' provenance.

got my bank to confirm the funds and got the train and stayed overnight near the auction house. I was convinced every UK and French dealer would be there and on the trains, and kept on looking around and behind me. No one. Not yet at least.

Fig.5.1 Catalogue page from the auction house in Orléans, drawing by Denys Calvaert

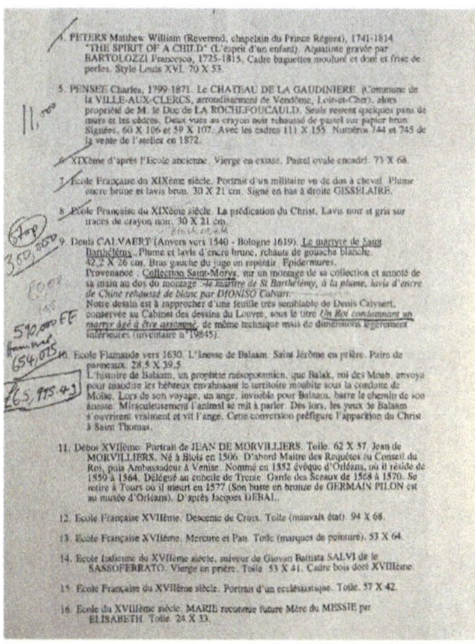

4. PETERS Mathew William (Reverend, chapelain du Prince Régent), 1741-1814 "THE SPIRIT OF A CHILD" (L'esprit d'un enfant). Aquatinte gravée par BARTOLOZZI Francesco, 1725-1815. Cadre baguettes mouluré et doré et frise de perles. Style Louis XVI. 70 X 53.

5. PENSEE Charles, 1799-1871. Le CHATEAU DE LA GAUDINIERE (Commune de la VILLE-AUX-CLERCS, arrondissement de Vendôme, Loir-et-Cher), alors propriété de M. le Duc de LA ROCHEFOUCAULD. Seuls restent quelques pans de murs et les cèdres. Deux vues au crayon noir rehaussé de pastel sur papier brun Signées. 60 X 106 et 59 X 107. Avec les cadres 111 X 155. Numéros 744 et 745 de la vente de l'atelier en 1872.

6. XIXème d'après l'Ecole ancienne. Vierge en extase. Pastel ovale encadré. 73 X 68.

7. Ecole Française du XIXème siècle. Portrait d'un militaire vu de dos à cheval. Plume encre brune et lavis brun. 30 X 21 cm. Signé en bas à droite GISSELAIRE.

8. Ecole Française du XIXème siècle. La prédication du Christ. Lavis noir et gris sur traces de crayon noir. 30 X 21 cm.

9. Denis CALVAERT (Anvers vers 1540 - Bologne 1619). Le martyre de Saint Barthélémy. Plume et lavis d'encre brune, rehauts de gouache blanche. 42,2 X 26 cm. Bras gauche du juge en repentir. Epidermures.
Provenance : Collection Saint-Morys, sur un montage de sa collection et annoté de sa main au dos du montage : *le martyre de St Barthélémy, à la plume, lavis d'encre de Chine rehaussé de blanc par DIONISO Calvart.*
Notre dessin est à rapprocher d'une feuille très semblable de Denis Calvaert, conservée au Cabinet des dessins du Louvre, sous le titre *Un Roi condamnant un martyr âgé à être assommé*, de même technique mais de dimensions légèrement inférieures (inventaire n°19845).

10. Ecole Flamande vers 1630. L'ânesse de Balaam. Saint Jérôme en prière. Paire de panneaux. 28,5 X 39,5
L'histoire de Balaam, un prophète mésopotamien, que Balak, roi des Moab, envoya pour maudire les hébreux envahissant le territoire moabite sous la conduite de Moïse. Lors de son voyage, un ange, invisible pour Balaam, barre le chemin de son ânesse. Miraculeusement l'animal se mit à parler. Dès lors, les yeux de Balaam s'ouvrirent vraiment et vit l'ange. Cette conversion préfigure l'apparition du Christ à Saint Thomas.

11. Début XVIIème. Portrait de JEAN DE MORVILLIERS. Toile. 62 X 57. Jean de MORVILLIERS, Né à Blois en 1506. D'abord Maître des Requêtes au Conseil du Roi, puis Ambassadeur à Venise. Nommé en 1552 évêque d'Orléans, où il réside de 1559 à 1564. Délégué au concile de Trente. Garde des Sceaux de 1568 à 1570. Se retire à Tours où il meurt en 1577 (Son buste en bronze de GERMAIN PILON est au musée d'Orléans). D'après Jacques DEBAL.

12. Ecole Française XVIIème. Descente de Croix. Toile (mauvais état). 94 X 68.

13. Ecole Française XVIIème. Mercure et Pan. Toile (marques de peinture). 53 X 64.

14. Ecole Italienne du XVIIème siècle, suiveur de Giovan Battista SALVI dit le SASSOFERRATO. Vierge en prière. Toile. 53 X 41. Cadre bois doré XVIIIème.

15. Ecole Française du XVIIème siècle. Portrait d'un ecclésiastique. Toile. 57 X 42.

16. Ecole du XVIIIème siècle. MARIE reconnue future Mère du MESSIE par ELISABETH. Toile. 24 X 33.

Fig.5.2 Catalogue page from the author's file with his bidding notes

I got to the auction house and asked to see the drawing, and within seconds I decided I would bid: yes it was in amazing condition and I was determined to buy it at the estimate of 200,000 French Francs.[66] The auction was on a Sunday, which was quite normal for auctions in rural France. Auctions are a spectacle for the town, and the townsfolk come to watch, wearing their finest clothes and hats. Not a drawing dealer in site. Now I was sitting there waiting for the drawing to come up watching for signs of other activity. The phone was being picked up about five lots before mine. Not a good sign. And then literally four lots before the bidding in walks Martin Grässle[67], from Munich, who partners with Katrin Bellinger. I knew I was toast. The drawing comes up and my heart sinks. My maximum bid literally passes in seconds to the phone bidder, and Martin go head to head, 400,000 French Francs, passes, 500,000 passes, and I am in a daze of disappointment. I didn't even get to raise my hand in a bid, the increments were going up so quickly. The bid settles at 590,000 French Francs, and even Martin was outbid. I knew who bought it,[68] well I had an educated guess, and was correct.

So, as a dealer, once you have your drawing you have to then pay for it. You then need to research it, and possibly have some conservation work done on it, and have a frame made or buy one, and then you need to present it for sale. So the fictitious drawing you have bought for sale at £5,000 now costs you £500 for the frame, £60 for the mount, and maybe £200 for the conservation. So you must sell it for £5,760 to break even. Now you are in the business of making money and you need to make a decent margin. Now the margin is the difference between the price you bought it and you sell it at, less VAT. Let's say you sell it for a modest profit, say a net price of £10,000, less your costs of

---

[66] Roughly £20,000-30,000

[67] Martin Grässle and Katrin Bellinger formed a formidable business partnership, dealing in Master Drawings. Katrin went on to own Colnaghi with Konrad Bernheimer, and they sold the business to Jorge Coll who now owns and runs the business.

[68] It was bought by Jean-Luc Baroni of Colnaghi, and the drawing was in their next catalogue, Colnaghi, *An Exhibition of Master Drawings* at Adam Williams Fine Art Ltd, 4 May-2 June, 2000, catalogue no. 13.

£5,760, and VAT at 20% of £888, so a margin of £3,512 for that time, expertise, effort and outlay of cash. What are the opportunity costs of that outlay of cash just sitting in a high interest or high earning investment account?

Now that is also assuming you sell it to a private collector who pays you on time. If you sell to a museum payment could be up to 1-6 months down the line. The cash flow for a dealer is not for the faint hearted. But what about your other costs? Exhibitions at art fairs need to be paid in advance, a website needs to be built, you need to live and pay your own household bills, you need to pay your salary for your staff or employees or short term staff. Also finding these objects is not easy, it can take a lot of time and effort to find the right objects to buy. No one needs art, it is a passion purchase. You cannot eat it or live in it. It is a discretionary purchase. Most of the costs for a dealer are front loaded and you only get paid after all these costs have been paid, and so the margins need to be high to make this work financially.

Another model: Art Fairs or Art Walks

Two other businesses I created were *Master Drawings London* and *Master Drawings New York*, and the business model and cash flow was almost the reverse to that of dealing.

All the income from fees came in before the event, and then the bills were paid. Much easier to run. I started *Master Drawings London* in 2000/ 2001 because I wanted collectors and clients to know about my art dealing business. I had my first exhibitions on Bond Street in 1999 and 2000[69] (see Fig. 6), and watched all these collectors, dealers and museum curators I knew passing along Bond Street and wondered why are they are not coming in? Do they know I have an exhibition on? Why are they not coming in since most people in this field are very curious about what is on the market. So I came up with the idea of

[69] Crispian Riley-Smith, at John Mitchell & Son, 160 New Bond Street, London, 28 June till 9 July 1999 and 15th June till 7th July 2000.

creating a common platform for the dealers to promote their exhibitions. I presented my ideas, with James Mitchell[70] at a lunch and invited all those dealers in London who I thought might be interested in showing, and had a take up of around 90% subscribing to the first event in 2001.

Fig.6. Author at an exhibition of "Master Drawings" at John Mitchell & Son, circa 2001

The mistakes I made in setting up this business, and indeed *Master Drawings New York* I touch on, but essentially it was a "win win" for dealers, collectors, the public, the press and the curious.

I find it interesting to note that most of the auction houses, dealers and art fairs are privately owned. Big corporations do not own them. That is because

[70] James Mitchell is a third generation art dealer, who now runs the gallery in London with his brother William Mitchell.

it is difficult to make money in this business. It is mostly private individuals who can appreciate the nuances of the Art Market, and who are willing to take the significant risks required. Large financial corporations find it too risky, which I find rather amusing considering the risks they take.

4

Chapter 4: How I started my First Art Business.

I remember vividly the joy of leaving Christie's and being my own boss. But I knew I had to get some real life experience under my belt as a dealer. I was nervous about buying, and started to work as a runner.[71] This was something my father encouraged me to do, but meant I went from one dealer to another and taking a drawing on consignment and offering it to another. I had some success but the margins were tiny and I was making hardly enough money to make it worthwhile.

I do remember taking some drawings by Alexander Nasmyth (1758-1840) for a Walter Scott Novel on consignment, when I was working as a "runner". I literally went into a gallery in Edinburgh and asked one dealer what they were looking to buy, and then went into another nearby who had drawings by the same artist. Simple, but the margins were small.

What to buy?

[71] A runner is the name given to a dealer who literally takes the object from one dealer to another and does not pay for the work. They metaphorically "run" from one dealer to another.

Now when I am asked, "what do you buy"? I say I know it when I see it. There is a very good summary given by the collector Jeffrey Horvitz [72] in an interview which explains his approach to buying, which I think sums up my buying system as well. But I would add a few nuances since when I was working as a dealer I also had to have a few of my own rules and desires. The rules or circles form a Venn diagram and consisted of these subjective rules: did I like the drawing and find it beautiful to own, this was key to me. It must strike a visceral cord– I like it, I want it, I must buy it; another one was could I make a profit on it? Because I liked it would other people like it? What is the condition like? As a dealer you learn what can be conserved and saved and what cannot. Drawings and watercolours which had faded- forget it. But drawings with heavy foxing could be brought back to life. Foxing is the discolouration on the paper surface, and is caused over time, and looks yellowish or reddish-brown spots. You have probably come across this in old books. Now sometimes if a drawing is laid down onto another piece of paper there is the added excitement that there might be a sketch on the verso[73]. Indeed this was the case with a drawing by Bandini which I sold to the Fitzwilliam Museum,[74] in Cambridge (see Fig.7).

---

[72] *Mastery & Elegance, Two Centuries of French Drawings from the Collection of Jeffrey E. Horvitz*, Margaret Morgan Grasselli, Jean-Francois Méjanès, William W. Robinson, 1999, pp.77-93

[73] Verso is the reverse or back of a drawing, and recto is the front of a drawing.

[74] Inventory number PD.3-2004

Fig. 7, Giovanni di Benedetto Bandini, called Giovanni Dell Opera (1540-1599), 2A Standing Figure of a Saint (recto and verso)", black chalk, pen and brown ink, 404 x 194 mm, The Fitzwilliam Museum, Cambridge

Now the funny thing was I had all these rules and guidelines to use when I bought an artwork, but when I sold it to a collector or dealer or museum their reasoning was almost always different to mine!

I thought the job of the dealer, certainly in the field of works on paper, which was the one I knew extremely well, was to make discoveries, or to add value. This could be making a literal re-discovery of an artwork that had lain unrecognised for a long time or by adding value to the artwork, by exposing it in a different light. I enjoyed doing both things. Indeed, I was quite good at making discoveries in this field, because I had spent so much time and effort in training my eye and researching drawings. Quite early on I made a rather exciting discovery by a 16th century artist working in Florence. This drawing was one I bought because I loved it, and it was one I studied for many years and is forever imprinted on my memory. When I bought it, I thought it was one of the most beautiful drawings I had seen. By that I would add a qualifying note -one that I could afford and find on the Art Market. It had been drawn with such delicacy, I was enthralled by it. I did not know who drew it, but I suspected it was from Florence around 1500-20. I also knew it was good quality. Several years later I did find a painting which I thought it was a preparatory drawing for, and it is called the "Pala della Signoria" which was an unfinished altarpiece by Fra Bartolommeo[75] . It was a eureka moment, and I was keen to see the painting when I was next in Florence. It was not by the Frate[76] but by an artist from the next generation.

So when I was next in Florence I went to visit the Museo di San Marco,[77]

[75] Fra Bartolommeo (1472?-1517), also known as Baccio della Porta, and Frate, since he became a Dominican monk in 1500.

[76] Fra Bartolommeo was a monk, and is sometimes called "Frate".

[77] Fra Bartolommeo (1472/74-1517), Unfinished Altarpiece "Pala della Signoria", monochrome oil on panel, 444 x 308 cm, Museo di San Marco, Florence.

where the picture is located today. To see this painting in the flesh was an amazing experience. From the catalogue it looked tiny in size and I don't think I bothered to look to see how big it was. I was also rather intrigued by its monochrome nature. I had one of those bizarre experiences in Italy when one arrives at the museum entrance on a day it is open and the guards say "chiuso", closed. Thankfully using my Italian I managed to get a brief entry to see this art work. What an experience. The museum is extraordinary since it is housed in the old Dominican convent where the monks used to live and pray, and in one of the monks cells is installed this stunning altarpiece. I was not prepared to see this massive and overwhelming painting standing over four meters in height. What a journey I had during my research.

I spent a number of years researching it, and showed it to a number of scholars. Eventfully one, Paul Joannides, said he was pretty sure it was a "juvenilia" drawing by Baccio Bandinelli[78]. This attribution was supported by Dr Roger Ward, who is the recognised scholar on the artist. It was the connoisseurship of Paul that made the connection. I sold the drawing to the American collector Jeffrey E. Horvitz, and he sold it at auction at Sotheby's New York 23 January 2008, lot 32,[79] (Fig. 8.1).

---

[78] Baccio Bandinelli (1493-1560), "Profile standing of a Saint Holding a Book", red chalk with traces of black chalk, red chalk counterproof (verso), watermark an encircled siren, Briquet 13886, Florence 1509, 282 x 160 mm

[79] Sold for US $52,000, including premium.

Fig. 8.1 Baccio Bandinelli, "Profile standing of a Saint Holding a Book", after Fra Bartolommeo, red chalk, 282 x 160 mm

Fig. 8.2 Fra Bartolommeo, "Pala della Signoria", monochrome, 444 x 308 cm, Museo di San Marco, Florence

Life on Bond Street.

I first met the Mitchell family when I was working at Phillips. Their business had been set up by their grandfather in the 1920s. James, William and I were similar ages and we became good friends. They asked if I would be interested in having exhibitions in their gallery and we worked together on an "ad hoc" basis for a few years. I had my first exhibitions as a dealer there.[80] This was fun since it gave me the opportunity to work with an established gallery, whilst retaining our own separate businesses. I got to meet their late father Peter, who was an expert in Dutch 17th century paintings and French 19th century pictures. I truly enjoyed working from their gallery and holding exhibitions there.

What does success look like?

Many dealers like selling to museums, and I was certainly one of them. I have sold works of art to The British Museum, department of Prints and Drawings and the department of Greek and Rome; The Getty Museum, California; The Metropolitan Museum, New York; Morgan Library & Museum, New York; The Wellcome Collection, London; The Fitzwilliam Museum, Cambridge; Statens Museum for Kunst, Copenhagen; The National Gallery of Art, Washington; The Art Institute of Chicago; Los Angeles County Museum of Art; Musée Goya, Castres to name a few. This is commercially counter productive since as a dealer you are taking these objects out of circulation in the market, unlike selling to a collector. I guess there was a certain vanity involved, in that as a dealer your style or taste was being endorsed by a museum or institution. Further it is an accomplishment that I am rightly proud of-finding works of art that are good enough to be in a museum.

After a number of years I had achieved much in the commercial world. I had

---

[80] 160 New Bond Street is at the corner of New Bond Street and Clifford Street, and is now a fashion house.

started my own art dealing business, indeed I had started two businesses more than I had originally intended. But I was still not achieving what I wanted to achieve. I think for a long time I had not given my aspirations any real thought. Whether this just needed time or maturity or some crisis to jolt me I just did not know. However I do suspect that I had not achieved the success I wanted to achieve because I did not believe in myself or my ability. This is not or a narrative that I now believe in. I do believe I can achieve great things, and will achieve the goals of setting up charities and trusts. I also want to continue to strive for a life that makes me happy and fulfilled.

For a long time I did not think I was worth this success. I could not achieve these goals, and listened to those demons in my head saying I could not do this. Now I believe and know I am capable of great things.

Many people underestimated me, and indeed I underestimated myself, but that is a big mistake, since I can dig deep and do things I never thought I could dream of or achieve. As someone said to me, "the biggest block in your life Crispian is you". Once you remove that you will soar. Thank you Ed for believing in me.

Discoveries in the field of Old Masters:

One of the main drivers in any market is the discovery nature of it. Discovering an artist, discovering a new technique, discovering more about how an artist works, discovering a new fact about an artist or the market, discovering ways to make money in a market, these are all drivers in a market. For me it was discovering art works. This takes time, effort, energy, resourcefulness, persistence, determination and luck. They say you make your own luck, which I do firmly believe.

I have made many discoveries in my career and some of the most exciting ones are not always the most financially beneficial. But knowledge is important and is hard won through study.

I once discovered a Jusepe de Ribera (1591-1652) drawing in a private UK collection, something I am especially proud of. I was in the collector's house going over the boxes full of drawings and the owner was in the other room and I stopped at this stunning drawing in a dark blood red chalk of a faun's head and I immediately thought of Ribera. The collector came into the room and I said I think this is close to Ribera, what do you think?

He said absolutely, please do research it. So I wrote to the expert on the artist's drawings, Gabriele Finaldi, now the Director of the National Gallery, London, and he first published the drawing in 2005[81]. I sold it in New York to a collector, and it was very satisfying all round. Whilst the drawing was on exhibition in New York, the other leading expert on the artist, Professor John Brown[82], came to see the drawing and gave it the thumbs up (see Fig. 9).

[81] G. Finaldi, "Dibujos inéditos y otros poco conocidos de Jusepe de Ribera", Boletin del Museo del Prado, 23, 41, (2005), pp. 24-44; and more recently published in "Jusepe De Ribera, The Drawings, Catalogue raisonné", 2016, pp.86-7.

[82] Professor John Brown (1939-2022) was an American Art historian, and in particular had expertise in Spanish art.

Fig. 9. Jusepe de Ribera, called Lo Spagnoletto (1591-1652), "The Head of a Man", red chalk, encircled watermark, 189 x 140 mm. Private collection.

Excitement of understanding a field and the discoveries

When I was finally able to unlock the secrets of connoisseurship and attribution it was very exciting to make those discoveries. It was almost like an addiction, the more I learnt the more I wanted to learn. I would go to museum shows, commercial exhibitions, art fairs, auctions, buy books, magazines and journals. For many years this was my focus, doing art shows in London, New York, Paris, Florence and Amsterdam. But this was all very costly taking art work across borders, staying in hotels, waiting for clients to come and then negotiate downwards or try and sell me their art works.

When I make a discovery of an artist it is because I can understand their technique. I would describe this skill in a simple way. I can easily recognise the hand writing of a close friend or a family member. I can recognise the writing on the envelope instantly. It is a bit like this when I look at a drawing. When there is no signature all I have to go on is the physical evidence in front of me. When I am in tune with an artist's technique I can recognise it. This comes from studying 10s to 100s of drawings by that artist. Of course some artists may not have that many drawings surviving in their whole output. The other evidence I have is the paper, and I can date paper from touching it and looking at the watermark and any inscriptions on the drawing or the mount. Usually this evidence is incredibly helpful, and this means taking the drawing out of the frame.

Mistakes and Failures

I have made plenty of them. That is okay. I do not mind falling over. A child learns to walk by falling over. And using the same analogy I learn by making mistakes. Indeed some businesses look to make mistakes, since they know they get to the next level through mistakes, and I completely buy into this philosophy. I embrace failure. I am not scared of it. I used to be terrified of failure, and this would make me procrastinate. I now hate to wait. By that I mean I am happy to wait in a queue, I am very English and love a queue.

Indeed if I see a queue I will join it. But what I hate is to wait for an idea not be to implemented. Over the years I have learned I need to stress test an idea, and will now refer this idea to more of my business advisers and team. Take this book, for example, now I have decided to write it I want it published, and hate to wait. The thought of going through a publisher and waiting another year would drive me crazy. Anything could happen by next year! No, I want this out by Christmas and I will get it out by then. I love the story of the first computers, some people wanted to wait until they had it just perfect. One American company said- who cares. Let's get it out to market and we will improve it, or correct it as we go along. What are we on now for the iPhone updates? Mine is now 18.6.2, this is literally the gift that keeps on giving for the company. My grandparents bought one fridge freezer, and this lasted them 50 years.

Wellness

This is not an area I priotitised until recently. Experience and life has taught me to really work on this on a daily basis. Work and the pressures of daily life take over in a way which you cannot expect or predict. But the key to all of this is your own health and well being. As they say in the introduction given by flight attendants to any flight, put your mask on first before helping the person next to you.

In the crises that I have experienced I often did not think about myself, but put my children or my business first and my own health and well-being second. This is not a great strategy for survival and the wheels will and do come off.

I have now found various strategies help me put myself first. One of them is doing a daily mediation and health programme. I try and always do at least 20 minutes of exercise. This takes me away from my computer and into the outside world. I love looking at trees and how the different leaves change in the seasons. Sometimes I feel I am looking at them for the first time, and wonder what I have been doing all these years. I like to go to the gym: it is like a mental trip on the bicycle, free wheeling down a hill. If I am feeling in a good mood I cannot understand why someone else is not feeling good. I have also been in those dark places of stress and anxiety and it is not a happy place. Running a business can be stressful, but it can also be fun. I think that change is inevitable. Businesses need to have a structural change every 10-15 years or sooner. Nothing remains the same. Amazon started off by selling only books, now it sells groceries and makes movies. As a business owner I need to be tuned into my tribe, and make the changes when it is necssary.

5

Chapter 5: How and why I chose my area of expertise

When I decided to focus on Old Masters as an expertise, I knew that it was going to be a long journey. Learning my skill. My father really encouraged me to choose an expertise. I was not interested in books and manuscripts as a subject matter, which was his interest, and the focus of his successful business. He had success selling Arabic books and manuscripts to the Arab market in the 1970s and in the 1980s, Economic books and collections to Japanese buyers. Many years later, upon his death, my brother and I were made partners of his book business along with our mother.

I was always drawn to what is called "flat art", rather than objects. I learn by visual images, and they fascinate me. I love films, I love reading. I was concerned that I liked watching too many films, but a wise person -Paul Joannides[83]- said to me that watching films was a great educator. I will take that advice.

Before I could do this I had to get a job after leaving St. Andrews University and

[83] Paul Joannides was married to the late Marianne Joannides, and was a University lecturer at Cambridge in the Art History department, and expert in Michelangelo and Raphael drawings.

had already started applying for the graduate jobs at Sotheby's, Christie's and Bonhams. Bonhams route to working in the expert departments was portering, which I didn't fancy, not because I was too grand to start at the bottom, but in those days they were by far in 4th place. The pecking order of auction houses, in the late 1980s, was Sotheby's and Christie's, then Phillips and then Bonhams. During the 1980s the Art Market was dominated by Christie's and Sotheby's, though things have now changed. Today I still work as a consultant to Bonhams in my core expertise of Old Master Drawings. My focus in 1988/9 was on Sotheby's, since I had already worked for the company and knew one of the directors in Florence, Julien Stock[84]. Anyway I applied for one of the five graduate trainee places, and during the last few months of university waited for a reply from Sotheby's. I think I had to call them to get an answer and the reply was "we are very sorry, you were the 6th choice, we are only taking 5". A few months later I got a letter saying that someone had dropped out and they were offering the place to me if I still wanted it. I was of course delighted and set myself for my first proper job after university. The market was buoyant with the Japanese dominance buying in the field of Impressionist and Classic Modern Art. Christie's had just sold Van Gogh's "Sun Flowers"[85] and the market was riding high. The rise of the Contemporary market had not really taken hold: that was to be in the next decades.

Sotheby's wanted their specialists to be generalists as well as specialists, so when specialists went into a property you looked at everything, and not just your area of interest. So I was moved around from department to department, and met some fascinating people. I started in the the Works of Art Department, where Lizzie Wilson,[86] was leading the department. It was in the basement of Ryder Street, opposite St. George's Church, and I loved the quirky medieval objects that landed in this department. It seemed that every object not wanted

---

[84] Julien Stock was an expert in Old Master Drawings and Paintings, and was Director in Florence and London.

[85] 30 March 1987, sale at Christie's of Van Gogh's "Still Life: Vase with Fifteen Sunflowers" to Japanese insurance magnate Yasuo Goto. It sold for a world record price of £24,750,000.

[86] Elizabeth Wilson ran the "Works of art" department which covered most hand made and machine made objects from 1400s till late 18th centuries.

by other departments ended up here. Of course the core expertise was bronze sculptures, and watching Lizzie handle and discuss these objects was inspiring. She clearly knew what she was talking about, and had handled a lot of objects over her 30 year career. Each day one of the specialists would bring in her dog to work, who was a rather sweet, if not rather smelly, springer spaniel. Quite bizarre. Sotheby's in those days was still very idiosyncratic. Even though the company was owned by Alfred Taubman[87] corporate America had not reached the works of art department. This is where I first met or rather saw the legendary Daniel Katz.[88] I then moved to the Silver Department, and the department was full of specialists in Continental and English Silver, and there were extraordinary characters who were specialists in heraldry and marks or stamps on silver. I attended a number of the silver auctions, and they were completely dominated by the trade. So much so that the lead buyer, Koopman,[89] would regularly buy 95% of the auction. I found this fascinating as well as bizarre.

Finally I got moved to some "flat art departments" and the money-making part of the auction business. They dominated the 1st floor on Ryder Street, and had the largest offices. I particularly liked meeting Michel Strauss[90], Melanie Clore[91], Helena Newman[92], and Adrian Biddell[93]. Michel's office was always clouded in smoke, those days you could still smoke in offices and on the tube-unbelievable really. I remember the auctions of spring 1990 when the Japanese withdrew from the Art Market overnight. The lead specialists

[87] Alfred Taubman (1924-2015) had bought Sotheby's in 1983.

[88] Daniel Katz is a dealer in Works of Art and has a gallery based in London.

[89] Jacques Koopman was one of the leading silver dealers in the 1980s and now the business is run by his descendents.

[90] Michel Straus (1936-2021) worked at Sotheby's for about 40 years and lead the Impressionist and Modern Department.

[91] Melanie Clore worked at Sotheby's for 35 years.

[92] Helena Newman still works at Sotheby's and is in a senior role as Chairman of Sotheby's Europe and Impressionist and Modern Department Worldwide.

[93] Adrian Biddell worked at Sotheby's for 27 years in the 19th century departments, and is now working at Olympia Auctions.

came into the offices after the auctions, saying "all estimates are now a third of what we have been previously quoting". In those days before the internet the estimates were based on previous auction records, which it is today, but in those days you had card indexes or The Art Sales Index, an annual two volume publication with the auction prices of fine art that had passed through the auction rooms. The bigger auction houses, and I have seen behind the façades of all four, all had different systems. Sotheby's and Christie's used card boxes, categorised by artist. My job, as an intern, was to take two auction catalogues and cut them up and paste these on to the cards. A specialist would say, get me the box on "Monet Hay stacks",[94] or "Picasso Blue period"[95]. The cards, with the recent auction records, would then be spread out in front of the specialists and the picture in question would be estimated, okay lets say £400,000-600,000. Next. And so this is how estimating is done! I remember Sotheby's Impressionist Department had two people constantly cutting up catalogues and pasting them onto cards.

On the graduate programme there were like-minded people including Mark Adlington,[96] David Breuer-Weil[97], and Rory Campbell[98]. The former two are artists today, but David also works as a dealer. The programme was run by James Stourton.[99] We did have some fun trips and there was one memorable trip to see the Saatchi collection, which at the time was in North London (Fig.10).

---

[94] Monet's series of Hay stacks were painted mainly at Giverny between 1890-91.

[95] Picasso's Blue period was between 1901-4.

[96] Mark Adlington is a contemporary wild life artist working as a painter, draftsman and sculptor, working in London.

[97] David Breuer-Weil works as painter, monumental sculptor and draftsman in London.

[98] Rory Campbell works as a lawyer in Belfast.

[99] James Stourton was at Sotheby's from 1979 to 2012, and now is an author.

Fig. 10. The graduate trainees after visiting the Saatchi collection in circa 1989, David Breuer-Weil, Rory Campbell, Mark Adlington and the author

I moved around to the department of Victorian and Modern British Art, where I remember spending weeks in the basement beneath St. George's Street, with Mark Adams[100]. I just seem to remember cataloguing the work of the 19th century decorative painter Alfred de Breanski (1852-1928), who was known for his paintings of highland cattle in landscapes, and he was a prolific painter. My abiding memory is cataloguing one painting after another, and trying to come up with another title for "Highland Cattle in a Scottish landscape". The "hilling sessions" or catalogue review sessions were when all the department members would get together and criticize or check cataloguing. This was what I enjoyed and dreaded the most. But this was why I was working in an auction house. Both Sotheby's and Christie's had a similar method of catalogue

[100] Mark Adams is a specialist in European Impressionism and 20th century Art, and works for an art advisory firm in London.

checking. Learning from other people. At Christie's this was called "hilling" because in the past when the cataloguing was checked in the basement of King Street the pictures were moved down the hill, hence "hilling". Bizarre, but that was the terminology at that firm. At Christie's this was normally fraught because Noël Annesley[101] would come and rip apart your cataloguing and ask have you sent it to this or that expert, have you checked this artist, or this book or have you thought of x, y or z. At the time he had already 30 years' experience in the business and had seen and made many mistakes himself, so this was of great use.

Going back to Sotheby's after the disaster of the collapse of the Impressionist market Sotheby's was going through another round of firings. I remember distinctly the one thing they did not cut back on was entertaining their clients. In the next marquee auctions they were preparing for the sale of the Hans Hoffman "Hare".[102] This was a painting which had been discovered in a house in Yorkshire and, as the story goes, had been used as a "fire guard". It was a panel painting, and for some reason, I guess because it was solid, it was used as a fire guard. Now it was being sold by Paul Josefowitz, who had bought it at Sotheby's in 1983, and the firm was going all out on the marketing of this painting. In the main rooms of Sotheby's a replica hare had been made as a centre piece for the banquet dinner, and the bottles of champagne were being piled up. This was in the same room that a few hours earlier many of the staff had been told they were about to lose their jobs.

I then got assigned to a totally different department, the jewellery department. Another money making department, which in those days was not housed in the main building, for obvious security reasons.

---

101 Noël Annesley started at Christie's in 1964, and was one of the longest serving directors and Chairmen. His expertise covers British and Old Master Drawings, and Prints.

102 The painting was exhibited well before the auction the following year to generate interest from buyers. It went unsold at Sotheby's, London, July 4, 1990, lot 14; but was then sold at Sotheby's, New York, January 25, 2001, lot 91, to the J. Paul Getty Museum.

I did enjoy working with the expert, Alexandra Rhodes, who was the Senior Specialist and Department Head when I worked there, and was frequently travelling to see clients. The International department head was the dynamic David Bennett[103]. They were all very pleasant and tried to persuade me to become a specialist, and take the gemmology exams. It was not for me and I decided to focus on getting a job in the Old Masters field. In some ways it was a great shame since I really liked all these specialists.

Time was running out, since my terms of employment at Sotheby's were not guaranteed. The graduate trainee position was for a year, and the hope was that I would be placed in a department during that period. I stayed on an extra six months in the jewellery department, hoping a position would come up in one of the departments I wanted to work in. Unfortunately in never did. So I left Sotheby's after 1½ years, and was spat back into the job market in 1991. The economy was in free fall, the first Gulf War was about to begin, and jobs were very thin on the ground- sound familiar to today? Interest rates were about to go to a dizzying 16%![104] I looked at other professions, such as accountancy or working in the city and it felt like I was forcing a round peg into a square hole. I always came back to what I really loved, however dire it all seemed economically. Old Masters or "Old Monsters" as some of my colleagues call it. Again was this another missed opportunity?

I widened my net and wrote to all the dealers in the field of Old Masters, and got interviews or chats with Derek Johns[105], Rafael Valls[106] who had their own firms carrying their names in St. James's and David Ellis-Jones[107] at

---

[103] David Bennett had a 40 year career at Sotheby's Jewellery division.

[104] Black Wednesday 16 September 1992.

[105] Derek Johns is a dealer in Old Master Paintings, and was based in the early 1990s in Duke Street, St.James's, and the business was called Harari and Johns.

[106] Rafael Valls is a dealer in Old Masters, and has had a gallery in Duke Street, St. James's, since 1976.

[107] David Ellis-Jones was a former director at Sotheby's and worked at Wildenstein when I met him.

Wildenstein,[108] which was still on Bond Street. This did pay off since I did got offered a job at Wildenstein at the same time as a job offer came from Phillips. It was a thrill to be offered a job by this venerable firm, and despite what has come out recently they were one of the great dealing businesses of the 19th and 20th Centuries.

Indeed some these of individuals and firms I would continue to bump into and work with, and often work as "half-share" partners when I became a dealer seven years later. "Half-shares" or as my father used to say, "halvsies", was a way that dealers reduce the risk in owning stock. The financial outlay can be significant, and as a business man or woman you want to reduce the risk. Also you can open up different clients if you have multiple owners. The problem can be sometimes the other "partner" can let you do all the work and selling, and they collect the cheque when the deal is done. In my experience there were swings and roundabouts with any business deal, and that was just part of doing business.

Anyway, this meant a lot of work and starting in a field that I knew from an academic position but could not distinguish a fake or a modern copy or the real deal. This meant years of going to exhibitions and studying. This area is huge, covering artists from around 1400 to 1930s, and countries including England, France, Germany, Netherlands, Spain and more. There is simply no way one could learn it all, so as a specialist you need to be able to navigate the field and know who the experts are and who to ask. I had to have a working knowledge of dating the age of the drawing from handling the paper, and which school the drawing was from. I literally spent the next 20-25 years studying the subject by going to museums, reading catalogues, and going to auctions. I did a rough calculation to see how many art works might have

---

[108] Wildenstein had a gallery in London until 1997, when the location was bought by Richard Green. The firm was founded in France in the mid 19th century, and has been owned by the family ever since, over five generations. They also established the Wildenstein Institute which publishes scholarly catalogue raisonnés . The family and the firm have been in various court disputes over tax and ownership issues.

theoretically been created during this period. There were many millions. How many drawings, paintings could have been created by artists, artisans and designers during this period. Let's say an artist has an average career of 30 years, and so from the age of 15 to 45. How many paintings, drawings and sculptures could they create in a day, a week, a year. Let's say 5 drawings a day so 1,825 a year, so 54,750 a lifetime, 450 paintings in a lifetime based on 15 paintings a year. How many artists are there in each generation? I know this is hypothetical, and much of what we have today has been lost or destroyed from previous generations. Think how much we throw out of our own working career?

Whether you focus on contemporary art or cars or ceramics the principles are the same. But it requires dedication and focus and commitment.

My ex-boss from Sotheby's, Julien Stock had been in contact, on my behalf, with one of the Keepers of Prints and Drawings at the British Museum, Nicholas Turner[109]. He, and his wife Jane,[110] were people I looked up to, and over the years I worked with them on many occasions. Initially Nicholas in his expertise on Guercino and later Jane in her role at the erudite and esteemed "Master Drawings Journal"[111]- but that was not for another 10-15 years.

My thinking behind working as a volunteer at The British Museum was that this was an entry into the world of "Old Masters", albeit these were pieces of paper, rather than paintings. This was not something I had ever really considered. I had seen the recent major Leonardo drawing show, in 1989, at the Hayward Gallery, which my Professor from St. Andrews University,

---

109 Nicholas Turner, worked at the Department of Prints and Drawings from 1974-1994 and the J.Paul Getty Museum from 1994-8.

110 Jane Turner was editor of Master Drawings Journal from 2004-24.

111 The Master Drawings Journal is a highly respected academic quarterly publication, published in America, since 1963. It is dedicated to publishing articles on drawings from 14th century to today.

Professor Martin Kemp[112] (Fig. 11), had co-curated. But more than that I had not really given it much attention. In all my years of being a student we had been to plenty of museums, but there had been no study of works on paper. I find this extraordinary since this is such a significant part of an artist's working process. Indeed as much as I loved university I did not find there was much practical real world experience, such as going to auctions or dealers or interaction with the Art Market.

Fig.11. Art History Graduates, 1989, St.Andrews University. Author in front row, middle, lying down. Professor Martin Kemp extreme right.

I agreed to work at the British Museum as a volunteer for two days a week, and

[112] *Leonardo da Vinci*, Hayward Gallery, London, 26 January to 16 April 1989.

I did telephone sales for the other days to keep money coming in. Working at the British Museum was like entering into a time warp, it felt like I was going back to the 1950s. Because the museum employees were part of the civil service, there were all these bizarre rules. For example, after 1 May, employees could wear short sleeved shirts; the keys to let you through the doors were dependent on the level of your civil service pay grade, since I was a volunteer this was the lowest; tea was served by a tea maid, going round with a trolley and biscuits, I kid you not. This was charming and also rather depressing after coming from the commercial cut and thrust of Sotheby's. I felt like I could die here and no one would discover my body for years. It was rumoured one of the paper handlers[113] would often sleep at night on the benches of the museum after having too much to drink. These were all stories circulating when I was there and I do not make any claim they are true, but it was funny.

When I started working at the British Museum as a volunteer in the Departments of Prints and Drawings it felt like I was entering an Aladin's cave. Indeed the space feels like a tomb or hall within a pyramid. And for anyone who has not visited this part of the museum it is like entering a huge swimming pool with a massive ceiling open to the natural daylight, since it is best to study prints and drawings in natural day light. This room is known as the "study room". Except there is no water in the middle, just rows and rows of books and 19th century cabinets stuffed with some of the world's greatest art works on paper. Period. There were so many places to start it was just where? So I started with Italian drawings, my main passion and obsession. So I pulled out the two volume of books written by two previous Keepers, the legendary duo, Pouncey and Gere, on Raphael and his circle,[114] and felt this was as good a place as any to start. This two volume book was my manual for studying and I would look at each drawing carefully and read what these two scholars wrote

[113] In those days there were "porters" or "paper handlers" who would bring your requested object to view from the cabinets to the tables, for you to examine and study.

[114] P. Pouncey and J.A. Gere, *Italian Drawings in the Department of Prints and Drawings in the British Museum, Raphael and his circle*, 1962.

on each drawing. It was a new language and fascinating to me. I was allowed free access to the cabinets, of course with another key. I started going through the thousands of drawings, looking and studying and trying to figure out and understand the creative process, and what each entry meant. It felt like a privilege to be up and close to Raphael and his circle, and learning new and complicated names of artists, such as Piero Buonaccorsi, called Perino del Vaga (1501-1547). It was and is thrilling, like standing on the shoulder of these great artists, staring down the centuries. For me this will always be an incredibly exciting moment. A few years later, when I first started dealing I sold a group of drawings by Vincenzo Brenna [115] to the British Museum and this was an incredible privilege. These were actually bought by the department of Greek and Roman, not Prints and Drawings. This was because the drawings depicted an imaginary re-construction of the Colosseum and Circus Maxentius.

I was keen to get back into the commercial world and after having worked at the British Museum for a few months, I got offered an interview with Phillips. I had written to the director of the Picture Department, Brian Koetser[116] and was asked to come in for an interview with Sarah Lidsey, who was the head of the department, and knew a lot about drawings and paintings from working in the department for many years and handling the objects. She showed me a number of drawings and asked me about them. This was after having worked for a few months at the Museum, and my knowledge was clearly very limited. She showed me one drawing which was a counterproof[117] (Fig. 12.2). I did not know what this was or what it meant. This was rather embarrassing since it is for all intents and purposes a photocopy. Albeit an 18th century version of photocopying. What the artist did was wet the back of the original sheet of paper with the drawing on it, usually with a sponge, and dampen the receiving

[115] British Museum acquisition numbers: 2010,5010.1 to 2010,5010.5

[116] Brian Koetser was a dealer in 1960s and 1970s and worked at Phillips and Bonhams, and is a leading specialist in Old Master Paintings.

[117] Attributed to Jean-Honore Fragonard (1732-1806), *Seated girl, leaning with folded arms on a sketchbook*, red chalk counterproof over traces of black chalk, within black ink framing lines, 288 x 228 mm

piece of paper. Then the original drawing was pressed against the new sheet of paper. This resulted in a copy of the drawing, which was a mirror image of the original. A copy with differences. The copied version would clearly be a mirror image of the original. Artists like Hubert Robert, and many 18th century French artists, would often do this multiple times, using the same original drawing. It worked best with red chalk drawings for obvious reasons. Artists liked this technique because it became part of the creative process, they would sometimes work up the drawing, or sell copies or just keep them. As an "expert or specialist" in drawings the tell tale characteristic was the "handwriting" of the drawing or the hatching stroke, would go from bottom right to top left in counterproofs. This was because 99% of artists are right handed, and the hatching strokes go from bottom left to top right in the original drawing. Only people like Leonardo and a few other artists are left-handed draftsmen. Anyway back to this drawing at Phillips, I felt I really had to up my game and learn more about drawings to understand this field.

Fig. 12.1.Phillips Picture Dept., New Bond Street, c. 1992: Back row: John Dabney, Charles Young, James Rawlin, Tessa Helfet, Sarah Lidsey, Victor Fauvelle, Sophie Money, Peter Romilly, author, Daniel Brooke; next row: Sarah Joyce; Sue Boyes-Korkis; James James Crook; Charlotte Maclean; Peter Arnold; Marcus Halliwell; seated: Richard Lloyd, Brian Koetser; Alexandra Gill, Arda Kassabian

Fig. 12.2. An example of red chalk counterproof, Bonhams, 7 July 2004, lot 65.

Back at the British Museum, when I started working there Nicholas Turner was putting the finishing touches to his catalogue on Guercino[118]. An artist I had never heard of before I started working there. But as I soon learned there were literally going to be thousands of artists I have never heard of and I needed to navigate this new world. Like many of the artists of this period they have two names, Guercino was his nickname. Literally "the squinter", which is not very sympathetic, since he did indeed have a medical condition. It is called congenital strabismus, meaning he was born with one eye that turned inward, see Ottavio Leoni's print "Portrait of Guercino". Indeed working on this exhibition and doing a deep dive into this artist was quite fortuitous, since it helped me tune into this artist, I made a number of discoveries of works by this artist over the years, including one at Phillips (Fig. 13.1 and 13.2).

This was a re-discovery, which made a worldwide record of £140,000 hammer price, and was the artist's auction record for about 10 years, was one I made from a private collection in Switzerland. What was exciting for me as an entrepreneur were the opportunities it gave me to be creative. I was thrown into the deep end, after about a year or two, and told to be a "business getter" and go and get drawings in for auction. This meant I was responsible for travelling in the UK, Europe and America, sourcing drawings for auction. I was working closely with a consultant. This I enjoyed very much and learnt a lot, working with the wonderful late Marianne Joannides. Marianne, and her husband Paul Joannides, became close friends and for a few years it was wonderful to work with them and learn from their wide experience and expertise.

The drawing in question was in a collection in Switzerland and I was on a trip with the amazing Nicolas Beurret[119], the Phillips representative in Zurich, who went on to run a very successful auction house in Switzerland. We went to the client's house to do a routine collection for sale. Indeed the client was

---

[118] N. Turner and C. Plazotta, *Drawings by Guercino from British Collections*, 1991

[119] Now trading as Artcurial Beurret Bailly Widmer

quite matter of fact, and said that this drawing was a period copy, and was happy to consign for sale for low £1,000s. Indeed this was quite rare since in my experience most clients would "big" up their collection, saying this was a masterpiece by Rubens or Rembrandt or Guercino.

The drawing in due course arrived in London. Before the auction there is usually a frantic few weeks, and months if you are lucky, spent researching and cataloguing each drawing, contacting experts for their opinions and such like. Marianne had been working on the drawing remotely and we both had come to a similar conclusion. This was either a period copy, and a good one, or was an original drawing by Guercino. Guercino drawings were being discovered at a rate of about 5-10 a year. I think that was what I had heard from Nicholas Turner, and so it was not such a stretch of the imagination to think this could be an original. I was taught that you always go back to the drawing. Is this good? Is this typical or characteristic of the artist? Here my lessons from Heatherley Art School came into play, see later in this chapter. This drawing was certainly good, and it was in red chalk, which was one of Guercino's favoured mediums. There was however something unusual about it. For the market to take this drawing seriously we needed to get the opinion of the specialist. In my experience it must be the expert who the market takes seriously and is listened to. In 1994/95 this was Nicholas Turner and Sir Denis Mahon. Both had just recently published the book on Guercino drawings at Windsor Castle.[120] So I sent a letter to my old boss at the British Museum, who was now at his post as Curator of Drawings, at the Getty Museum in California. It was not surprising that his reply that came back was he was not able to comment, due to his new role. This was fair enough so we wrote to Sir Denis, who was very prompt in his reply, and came into the office to see the original drawing. It was a real privilege to meet this kind gentleman who had worked so hard to restore the reputation of Bolognese art for the last five decades. He had written that he used to buy drawings from the mid 1930s to mid 1960s,

---

[120] D. Mahon and N. Turner, *The Drawings of Guercino in the Collection of Her Majesty The Queen at Windsor Castle*, 1989.

by Guercino for about £5, since it was cheaper to buy the drawings and study the artist, than to have photographs made, which was an expensive process in the 1930s. His collection of drawings is now in the Ashmolean Museum, Oxford.[121] When Sir Denis came into the office, he looked at the drawing, and said in his clipped voice, words to this effect "yes this is indeed by Guercino, and a late drawing, from the 1650s. The reason you will have trouble finding a comparative is that there are not many in the UK, there are some in the US", and directed us to a number of comparisons.

[121] They were placed there on long term in 1984, and acquired in 2012 through the UK Government Acceptence in lieu scheme. There are 46 drawings by Guercino, one by his nephew, Cesare Gennari, and two by Sir Joshua Reynolds, after Guercino.

Fig. 13.1 Guercino, *Susanna and the Elders*, red chalk, 305 x 332 mm, sold for world record,

Fig. 13.2 Cover of the auction catalogue, lot 149

The drawing was sold for a world record that summer, and it was a bittersweet moment since I could not be at the auction, becasue I had moved on to a bigger auction house: Christie's. And that is another story and journey of learning.

Working at Phillips from 1991 through 1995 was a unique time as the company was still incredibly old fashioned. All letters were written by a pool secretary, and she was shared with about ten specialists in the picture department. There were four copies of each letter, one for the client, one for file, one for the directors, and I cannot remember who the fourth one was for. It was bonkers. I wanted to write them myself, but I was not given a computer for a while. Indeed there is a photo of me with one the strangest looking computers in the background, (Fig.14.1). The company was owned at the time by Christopher Weston[122], a very charismatic businessman. It was still all very traditional and a full breakfast could be had on site, plus lunch. I am sure I gained a lot weight during my employment at Phillips. We left at 5:00 pm on the dot, and if we happened to be there after 5:00 pm the joke was to answer the phone with the phrase "night porter". I am not sure we did, but we had a lot of fun. This was a far cry from the world of Christie's, which was yet to come, which was the polar opposite.

There were funny stories of rushing down to the "crusher" in the Haunch of Venison yard. This was literally a mechanical crusher of wooden crates and boxes, which was a permanent fixture on the tarmac. I remember often running down to check the boxes before they got put into this machine, because we would unpack crates from the extensive regional offices both in the UK and abroad with items for sale. Sometimes objects and pictures were lost and this would be our first port of call.

When I worked in the Old Master's department at Phillips, which is now the Bonhams location, we had a number of successes. One of them came in four drawings by the Florentine artist Jacopo Ligozzi (1547-1626) (Fig. 14.2) they

[122] Christopher Weston was Chairman and Chief Executive between 1972 and 1998 of Phillips, Son & Neale.

sold on 7 July 1993. These four drawings of stylised female heads were not only incredibly beautiful to look at, they were very rare on the market. So when four came up for auction at the same time the small world of Old Master Drawings was electric with the news. On the day of the sale, and indeed minutes before the auction a call came in saying the lot numbers did not match the description. This was because during the proofing stage the images looked better on the double page spread with the women facing each other (Fig. 14.2). But we had not swapped the descriptions, because "back in the day" the catalogue was literally put together by creating a dummy physical catalogue with A3 sheets and the images and descriptions were cut and pasted with glue onto the A3 sheets. This resulted in a very messy proof being given to the printer. I came up with the last minute solution of issuing a saleroom notice to say the lot under the image was the lot being sold. This was because I knew 99% of buyers would make their decision on the image, not the description. The global low estimate was £40,000, for all four, and they all sold for £299,000, hammer price. Just recently one of the original set of four sold for $US 504,000.[123]

[123] Christie's New York, 4 February 2025, lot 18, sale price includes buyer's premium.

Fig. 14.1 The author in Phillips office, New Bond Street, London, with one of the Jacopo Ligozzi heads

Fig. 14.2 Two of the Ligozzi heads, as they appeared in the catalogue, opposite each other

I remember fondly the store house at Phillips, which was next to Haunch of Venison Yard, in which all the uncollected lots from sales would be placed. It looked like something out of Dickens, with racks upon racks of uncollected pictures, with dust collecting on them, and some of the pictures going back decades.

When I decided to focus on Old Master Drawings as a specialist, Christie's was the auction house to work in. It was the market leader, even more so than Sotheby's. Many of the major auctions in the last 30 years, in this area of specialism, had taken place at Christie's. This really started with the Chatsworth Auctions in 1984[124] and 1987, Holkham Hall in 1991, not to mention their auctions in Amsterdam, Monaco and New York. The Chatsworth auction revolutionised the market of Old Master Drawings, and opened it up to a much bigger group of collectors.

I had already applied to Christie's for their graduate programme in 1989 and had a brief interview with Noël Annesley, and Lord Carrington[125]. It was short, since I was already about to be employed by Sotheby's, but I thought it was a good idea to keep in with them, just in case.

Anyway after I left Sotheby's for the next five years I had written to Noël every year, asking for another interview.

As it happened when Nicholas Turner had gone to the Getty Museum, a specialist from Christie's, Hugo Chapman[126], had moved to the British

---

[124] *Old Master Drawings from Chatsworth*, 3 July 1984, and *Old Master Drawings from Chatsworth*, 6 July 1987; *Old Master Drawings from The Ian Woodner Collection*, 2 July 1991; *Old Master Drawings from Holkham*, 2 July 1991; *The Hans van Leeuwen Collection*, Part I and Part II, 24 November 1992.

[125] Lord Carrington, 1919-2028, was a British Politician and Chairman of Christie's from 1988-1993.

[126] He is Keeper of the Prints & Drawings Department, at the British Museum, and was Assistant Keeper of Italian and French drawings from c. 1400 to ca. 1800

Museum. Which is the art world equivalent of musical chairs and meant an opening came up at Christie's in the department I wanted to work in. I wrote to Noël again and this time I was asked to come for an interview. Of course I was meeting Noël with some trepidation, since he had a formidable reputation. I was called into his office and after some brief pleasantries he pointed me to various drawings, or photographs of drawings, on his wall. Of course, I knew they were photographs this time- I was not going to repeat the school boy error I had made with Sarah Lidsey, when I did not know what a counterproof was.

He pointed me to one particular drawing, of a saint reclining on an arch, and asked me had I seen it before, and I said no, which I hadn't. He then said what did I think and I said it looked near Michelangelo, I paused and then said possibly around Sebastiano del Piombo. He was silent for an extended period, clearly something had disturbed him, which made me very nervous. He said how do you know? I said I just do, and that is where I would look. He said that it had taken him three weeks to find the attribution, and looked rather peeved. I did not realise how important this was to him at the time. Twenty-five years later he had the image of this drawing used on the invitation to the Morgan Library dinner (Fig. 15.1 and 15.2) which was honouring his contribution to the field and his scholarship. There was a whole back story, which I of course knew nothing about, and when it had sold in 1977[127] it had made a record price, and was given to the National Gallery of Art in Washington in 1985. Fast track 25 years later I reminded Noël of this interview when we met at the reunion dinner, and he said "well that was why I employed you"! At the dinner there were a number of past and present employees of Christie's (Fig. 15.1). Including me.

---

[127] *A Prophet Addressed by an Angel*, sold at Christie's London, 5 April, 1977, lot 43. Now National Gallery of Art, Washington, accession number 1985.40.1

Fig. 15.1 Master Drawings Journal dinner to honour Noël, 2020: Back row: William O'Reilly, Stijn Alsteens, Benjamin Peronnet, Jonathan den Otter, Furio Rinaldi, Florian Härb, Noël Annesley, Harriet Drummond, Nicolas Schwed, Ketty Gottardo, Johan Bosch van Rosenthal, the author, Jennifer Wright, Mrs Caroline Annesley, Annabel Kishor, Hélène Rihal

Fig. 15.2 Drawing by Sebastiano del Piombo, now in the National Gallery of Art, Washington

The move to Christie's was a classic art move disappointment, much harder work for almost the same remuneration as Phillips. And this was typical, indeed I recall having to negotiate extensively to get the same benefits as what I was on already.

On my first day at Christie's I arrived before 9:00 am and left at around 10:00 pm, getting home to Clapham around 11:00 pm.

I was thrown into the deep end with the Summer 1995 auction catalogue to finish. Which was ironic since when I left Phillips this was all but completed for the Phillips summer auction catalogue. Anyway I was told to write the entry on a "Head" by François Boucher for the summer sale.[128] This was a steep learning curve since this deep level of research was not something I had done. Anyway I quickly picked up the skill and used it throughout my career as a specialist in an auction house and as a dealer.

This was how it carried on for the next three years. It was like I was working in a merchant bank, but without the pay, or even prospects of significant pay. We literally worked weekends, nights, and worked on auctions in London (King Street and South Kensington), Amsterdam, New York and Monaco. Also there were the massive valuations and donations going to museums. The Weld-Blundell collection going to the Walker Art Gallery, Liverpool[129], the Suida Manning collection going to Texas,[130] and the countless photograph valuations which would come in by the tray load every day. This was my responsibility. Trying to get François Borne to sign off on these was impossible, partly because he was permanently travelling, trying to get in works for sale, and when he was in the office he was on telephone calls or "hilling" and was frankly too exhausted to go over the photos. He had to see everything, so these would pile up.

---

[128] Christie's London, *Old Master Drawings*, 4 July, 1995, lot 133.

[129] X. Brooke, *Mantegna to Rubens, The Weld-Blundell Drawings Collection*, 1998.

[130] Robert and Bertina Suida-Manning collection of 400 drawings, sold to the Jack S. Blanton Museum of Art, College of Fine Arts at the University of Texas at Austin.

Indeed I remember one particularly grim evening when we were all working late and François was showing a client the drawings coming up for sale. When François, literally collapsed and fell like a tree trunk next to the raised cataloguing table. Thankfully he did not hurt himself or hit his head on the benches. He jumped up and just carried on. It was like we were not allowed to say how tired or exhausted we were. Just insane.

This was not unique in how staff were treated, and most just put up with this. I imagine this has significantly changed. At the time it was common to hear of other friends and colleagues experience similar issues at other auction houses. I guess I should have stood up to and refused to follow the herd, but I didn't. That is another lesson I have had to learn. At the time I did not feel that I could stand up to and confront this issue. I was not confident enough in my own ability or myself. I was just a junior cataloguer. The attitude at the time was you were privileged to be offered a position at this firm, and if you did not like it you could go elsewhere. I think that once the red lines were crossed, for example I worked all the waking hours I could physically do, I could not roll this back. Therefore I felt I had a binary choice, leave and set up the business I wanted to set up, or stay and continue to work in this unhealthy environment. Of course there were other choices, but I did not seriously consider them. Again a fork in the road and I chose a certain path.

When at Phillips I had fought hard to get every consignment of drawings for auction, at Christie's we were literally drowning in drawings. In one early collection from a deceased London dealer's estate, the drawings were in their thousands, and the piles and piles of drawings were overwhelming. We were literally wading through them in the department. It was said that for decades the collector/ dealer had bought every lot of drawing for under £100 at all the London auctions in the 1940s through to the 1970s, before the market changed in the 1980s.

There were many postive benefits of working at Christie's. I got to see and handle many amazing drawings. I had a common interest with other specialists. I worked with some very clever people. Nicholas Schwed is particularly interesting, and one collector described him very well, saying "il mange les dessins": literally he had such a passion for the subject he "ate the drawings". I was constantly impressed by his incredible passion and knowledge for drawings. Working in such proximity and so intensely for hours on end can be very formative. He now runs his business from Paris and I enjoy seeing him whenever I am there.

Other figures included Francis Russell,[131] Florian Härb[132], and Johan Bosch van Rosenthal[133], who ran the drawings auctions in Amsterdam. I was assigned to be the "Dutch" liaison and from this started my passion for Dutch drawings and my specialist interest in and collecting this period, especially drawings from the 18th and 19th Centuries. As a dealer I found this area to be under sourced, and made some great sales, especially one to the Getty Museum of a drawing *Landscape with Cattle, Sheep, and Herders* by Jacob van Strij, see photograph of it being exhibited by me (Fig. 16.1)[134]

[131] Francis Russell worked at Christie's for over 40 years, is an expert in British and Old Master Pictures, and author.

[132] Florian Härb is an expert on Giorgio Vasari and dealer in Old Master Drawings.

[133] Johan Bosch van Rosenthal has his own Art Advisory firm in Amsterdam.

[134] Sold in 2008 to Getty Museum, their inventory number 2008.61

Fig. 16.1 The author with his mother at a "pop up" exhibition at the Royal Academy, London, Print Fair, Drawings section, circa 2005. See Jacob van Strij's drawing of "Cattle", now in the Getty Museum, on the left wall, centre.

Fig. 16.2 Selection of catalogues and printed material by the author in the running of his dealing business in Master Drawings

Equally at Phillips I worked with some amazing people, Andrew McKenzie[135], Sarah Lidsey[136], Richard Lloyd[137], and James Rawlin[138]. In such a small industry it was easy to make great friends, and I was sad to move on and not see much of them since my life changed into different working orbits.

At Christie's I was learning a huge amount about how to approach researching drawings, and go into a deep dive into provenance research as well as the literature. It is extraordinary how much one can find, and it is like searching for threads or nuggets of information. When you do find some primary material this can lead into a whole gold mine of information. This was something I had not really learnt at Phillips, since my main job was business getting, basic cataloguing, preparing the sales and training my "eye". You hear this word a lot in the Art Market, "he/she has a very good eye". What people mean by this is often quite varied, but in the world of Old Masters what this meant was they spent a lot of time looking at drawings, paintings and sculptures, or whatever discipline you refer to. At Phillips I learnt how to look. I owe a lot of my ability to Brian Koetser, who headed the picture department, and who encouraged me to do two things. Go back to art school, and learn again how difficult it is to draw, and have empathy with the artist. I took this advice and attended Heatherly Art School in Fulham. I went to the life drawing classes in the evenings after work, and found this new perspective interesting. I would try and imagine what it would be like to be an artist from the 16th or 17th centuries, using awkward materials such as steel nibs and chalk that crumbled, unlike the amazing tools we have today. I did enjoy learning how to draw again, and see my work from a different view. The art teacher was incredibly encouraging, and no matter how poor the drawing was she was so positive! Just wonderful, and I loved her comments. I have found in life that

---

[135] Andrew McKenzie worked at Bonhams and Phillips in his expertise in Old Masters and British Paintings, and is an author on Scottish history.

[136] Sarah Lidsey worked at Phillips and Christie's as a specialist in Old Master Paintings.

[137] Richard Lloyd worked at Phillips and then Christie's in the Print Department.

[138] Jame Rawlin worked at Phillips, Bonhams and Sotheby's as a specialist in Modern British Art, and now as a dealer.

being critical to someone close to you or who you are teaching is not helpful, and does not help them learn. Indeed it does the opposite. I think I am often my harshest critic, and I understand this is the same for most people, and I know if I have not done something well or not up to my standard, I just need to learn. I do not think we give enough consideration to just how difficult it was to do the physical act of creating art in the past.

The other piece of advice Brian gave me was to cut up auction catalogues and create a filing system and memory bank, see photographs of my filing system, see Fig 17.1.-4. What this did was create a massive visual imagery system in my head. By looking at auction and dealer catalogues and making a mini "Witt Library"[139], this meant that over a period of time my visual memory muscle was trained to recognise and memorise images. This takes a lot of work and patience. But I did this for about four years, in the evenings after work. I found that my visual memory grew exponentially. So much so that I can go around most museums and art collections and private collections and place the artist, date, country and subject matter. I also learnt that I had an ability to memorise and recall images, which meant I could remember an image I had seen in an auction catalogue or a book, even if I saw it many years ago. It is a bit like train spotting in the Art Market. This was incredibly satisfying that my visual knowledge could grow and develop.

139 The Witt photographic library consists of about 2 million images of paintings, prints and drawings from 1200 to 2009. It is part of the Courtauld Institute of Art.

Fig. 17.1 Author's filing of photos, notes on sale prices and other observations

Fig. 17.2 Author's photos on artists

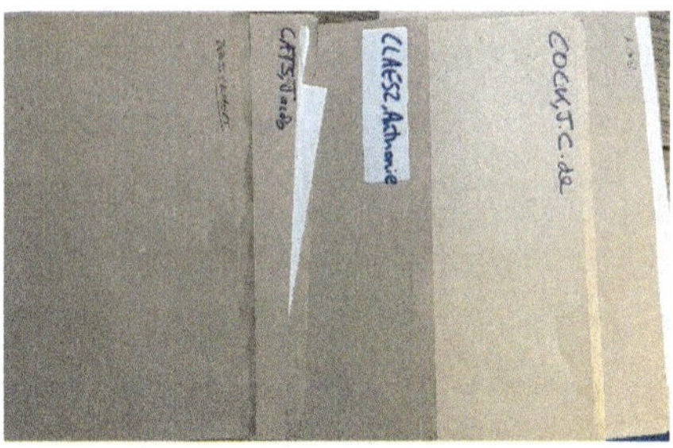

Fig. 17.3 Author's files on individual artists

Fig. 17.4 Author's boxes of photos, creating a mini "Witt" Library

At Phillips I was being presented with many drawings to value and evaluate on a daily basis and I needed to make a decision, was this worth researching or not? Smart phones did not exist, and it was not a thing to pull out a camera and take photos of drawings. This seems strange looking back, but this was how it was in my experience. These decisions had to be made quickly and with the drawing in front of me. So it was important to understand what was quality? Indeed if you have seen some of the sketchy drawings by Nicolas Poussin (1594-1665), or indeed Claude Lorraine (c.1600-1682), you would be amazed at how poor they look. A number of years later, when I was dealing, I made a discovery of a Claude drawing because it looked so weird. Many other dealers and auction houses had overlooked it. But as a specialist you need to understand the variety of techniques. There were many lessons I learnt in those four years at Phillips and three at Christie's. Another was never ignore an inscription, however bizarre it might be. Be open minded to what an artist can achieve. A Michelangelo drawing on a bad day is a very different beast to Michelangelo on a good day. I find it fascinating that Michelangelo is known to have burnt many of his drawings, and Vasari mentions that he "burned a large number of his own drawings, sketches, and cartoons so that no one should see the labors he endured and the ways he tested his genius, and lest he should appear less than perfect". Michelangelo held bonfires in his garden in Rome. There are contemporary accounts of people saying what is that fire? Oh it is Michelangelo burning his drawings. What has come down to us is probably 5% of his output. He was controlling his legacy. Whilst I find this upsetting as an art historian and collector, I completely get it. I do not want to keep my old notes and files from school or university and would burn these quite happily. The same is said about Francis Bacon. He is known to have drawn, but denies it, and there are various stories circulating of him destroying his work, and in one of these versions Bacon is said to have bought back one of his drawings from a gallery and destroyed it outside the shop. He is known to have destroyed many of his paintings, editing what his legacy looked like. Caravaggio (1571-1610) is not known to have done any drawings, and I suspect some of this has to do with the fact that he was always on the move!

After working at Christie's for 3 years I reached the point where I felt I did not have a longterm future with the company. I knew enough of the business to know that there were culls of the specialists, and these were brutal. I had seen it at Sotheby's in 1989 when the market crashed, and this was repeated again and again. Now in 2025 the auction houses have again in the last 2 years seen some massive reduction of their staff. When I wrote my letter of resignation at Christie's I was surprised to be offered a place in another of the departments at the firm, the books and manuscripts department, which was not something I had expected at all. Again another junction in the road. I chose to be a dealer rather than stay with an auction house. It was just a matter of time before I would be let go. The long term future in an auction house is in management, which did not interest me because I wanted to start my own business.

I was also impatient to start my own business. So I left my last full time employer on 6 February 1998. This was a major step into the commercial world and a path I have stayed on. For the last 27 years I have had to earn my living on my wits and ingenuity.

Change will happen in the Art Market, and I have seen this in the 37 years I have worked in the business. When I started there were individual firms that were dominant, such as Ackermans, Mallets, Leger Galleries, Tessiers and Heim Gallery, to name a few. Now these have all gone. Why? Were they badly run, did the market change or did they not see it? Change happens in all industries, and the important thing for an entrepreneur is to be ahead of the curve, and see where that change will be before it happens. What about Blockbuster and Virgin Records? The former ignored the fact change was coming, the latter embraced it. I have heard it said that as a business you need to change your model every 10 years. Now I am not so sure about this, but I do know a few certainties. Change will always come, and as a business owner I need to be receptive to it and be on that curve.

At the moment I feel we are standing in a similar place to the mid 1990s. AI [Artificial Intelligence] is a bit like the arrival of the internet. We know it is coming; actually it is here already, and we know it will be big, but we do not know how big and quite how it will affect us and how we can apply it to our businesses.

I did not see the changes in my market, or rather I chose to ignore them and carry on. Not any longer. The new technology is here, and coming apace; so is digital art. Most of this new technology is being practiced by artists and bought and sold by artists and collectors. I find this fascinating since it also opens up different markets. Those collectors buying digital art[140] are not the traditional Art Market clients. The expereince of going to museums and seeing art works is changing. Tens of thousands of perople go to see immersive exhibitions on Van Gogh[141]. I see that I must embrace this change and go with it. Those collectors coming into the market are going to be collecting very different objects to their parents and grandparents. That is fine: collecting changes; people change. As a child I used to collect cards from cereal packets, and then the chocolate "After Eight" wrappers, now I collect works on paper, and in a few years I will move into something else.

---

140 Digital art is the term used to create art using digital technology, and can exist in various forms both psychically and on screens or other mediums.

141 The Musée d'Orsay in Paris had a VR (Virtual Reality) and AI exhibition, *Van Gogh's Palette,* which had a record attendance of almost 800,000 visitors to an immersive exhibition.

6

Chapter 6: Recognising the risks in a precarious world

When I left Christie's to set up my own dealing business I was not fully aware of the risks, and did not fully look into them. I did not do enough planning. Mistakes were made in the structure process and some would come home to roost years down the line. Unlike when I set up my businesses as a child selling daffodils and a nightclub as a student. This was a classic mistake this entrepreneur made of just wanting to get it started and moving, and I would some how work it out as I went along.

Risk is at the heart of any business. You must understand your attitude to risk. Like one of those forms you complete when you are asked: what are your views to risk, low, medium or high? I am not talking about putting all your money on red or black or the number eight on the roulette table. This is much more nuanced, and has a longer tail, but does carry with it a lot of baggage- what are you risking? What are you prepared to risk and suffer for what you want or believe in? When you set up your own business you do the following whether you like it or not:

Give up a regular job
Your pay cheque

Your pension
Your support network at work
No guarantee you will succeed
No timeline to guaranteed success
No turning on email notifications and saying you are "on annual leave"
No one to blame, not your boss (since you are the boss), not your co-workers
Nowhere to hide
Difficult to get a mortgage
No regular holidays
Work from home
If you are ill there is no income, no sick pay, no movement in the business

The skills you will need to learn are endless, and there is no more calling up the technical support department and asking them to sort out your computer. You must become well versed in accountancy, bookkeeping, websites, VAT, import taxes, export taxes, people management and social media. You will have to develop skills you did not know existed! You will not be able to refer the problem to someone else! You will need to be a good communicator. I felt comfortable in the company of art, artists, museums and exhibitions. Why do some people prefer to communicate in some ways rather than others? I think I am a good communicator, but I was not always this way. I do remember feeling painfully shy when speaking to people, even as an adult. But by getting out there and speaking publicly and forcing myself to go up to strangers at networking events and introducing myself, I am now much better at this. My confidence has grown. I think I need to be out of my comfort zone to grow. Now I am learning Tik Tok. Now I will happily speak publicly given any opportunity. For a long time I did not have the confidence to say how I really felt. Now I do believe that what I have to say and do will help people and is relevant. That is another reason why I have finally written this book.

I think my appetite for risk is high, and this is fine, but I did not do this stress test on myself.

So if the risks are so high then what are the rewards? Surely these must be high? Well that is no guarantee. The guarantee is there is no guarantee.

The rewards for working for yourself, owning your own business are:

Independence
Money
Freedom
Pride of creating something
Taking your own path
The successes are all yours

All the success, and all the failures, of your hard work are yours. You have the freedom to choose what you do with your time, you get to work on your own schedule, and as hard or as little as you would like. I have been doing this for over 27 years and I feel that I have not taken off much time for myself. At times I have worked so hard, for so many years, I asked myself countless times was it worth it? Yes, I am in charge of my own schedule but I have always been thinking and worrying about work. At times this feels like a burden, and there were many times I have just wanted to run away from it all and find a job that took all this away. But I have always come back to the fact this is where I have laid my stall, I have made this bed and I have to lie in it. Not like some punishment but this is what I am good at, this is where I have made money. Switching career and focus is not going to convince anyone, and not me either. The skills I have gained over the last 37 years are unique to what I am doing now. I also recognise that I must be doing something right, since I have supported my family and myself for all this time. I may not have made as much money as some people I look at, but money comes and goes, and happiness comes from within.

At times, when I am doing well or have a new idea or feel I am moving in the right direction I feel alive, and that I can get to make a difference, and do all the things I want to do. When I sell an object and make a significant amount of money I am thrilled. However, as a dealer this was often short lived since I was drowning in other expenses. Anytime I made money I had to put the money back into stock or pay another fair or put the money into our house and pay down a mortgage or pay school fees. For these reasons I have wondered whether dealing was for me.

When I set up *Master Drawings London* -which grew into *Master Drawings and Sculpture Week* and then eventually *London Art Week*- I started a business model which was repeated many times in many cities across the world, and was one that many dealers and auction houses wanted to be a part of. Dealers and auction houses saw that it attracted clients, and buyers and Press and PR. They realised it reduced their costs of exhibiting at art fairs. For a number of years it was very successful, but repeating the same formula year after year became very difficult, like a treadmill and the movie "Groundhog Day".

Forming and running the art fairs was incredibly satisfying, and I am very proud of what I achieved. But I did not make much money from it and whilst it certainly helped my dealing business and my profile, it was not very profitable.

The same could be said for *Master Drawings New York*, which I set up in 2006 with Margot Gordon. I ran this for 16 years and sold the business to Christopher Bishop[142].

I found one of the results of being an entrepreneur is stress. I am now very focused on stress management because for too long I ignored this, which can lead to some health issues, and did for me. I am grateful to say that I am out of it, and feel much healthier and motivated as a result of the work I have done on managing it, and putting things into perspective. But I see the results of stress and anxiety every day with my colleagues. This can effect everyone whether they be an entrepreneur or an employee.

---

[142] Christopher Bishop's business, Christopher Bishop Fine Art, is based in New York, on the Upper East of Manhattan.

Problems and crises

I find that problems and crises come when you do not expect them. You need to know yourself and know how you might react. I have found that there is a pattern to my behaviour and I react in a certain way to extreme stress and problems. Firstly I would say I must have a high tolerance to stress, since I have had a number of stressful situations and in one period of my life I was dealing with multiple issues for about three years. I am very proud of myself for coming through them and becoming stronger and more resilient, and hopefully have become a better person to myself and my family and those I interact with around me.

I found stress is triggered by money, workload and family issues. I know these are my triggers and I know that I tend to withdraw upon myself, and turn the problem over and over in my head. The result is I withdraw into my primitive brain and do not use the creative side of my brain. As a result I can make poor decisions and ignore opportunities and withdraw in on myself. When I am firing on all four cylinders I am excited about the future and I am open to opportunities. I feel the moments of time with extreme clarity, and in some ways I feel I can see the future, like that film "Lucy"[143] where Scarlett Johansson consumes information like an AI machine and turns into a super computer. Life is good. I notice small things like the way a wild rose is blossoming on the hedges, or a skein of geese are flying over and am amazed how the geese swap over like they have a rota. When I am in a high stress mode everything becomes very hard. The days when I can do 100 things disappear. I struggle to complete three tasks and am tearful and angry with myself. But it takes time to understand myself, and why this occurs, and I have sought help over the years, and am extremely grateful that I can manage this nine times out of ten when a crisis comes. Because I can guarantee you a crisis will come. For me it was divorce, the death of my father, money. These were triggers and all could have been predicted, in one way or another. It is just how I handled them which matters.

---

[143] "Lucy", 2014, written and directed by Luc Besson.

I am proud that during my extreme crisis I moved from Yorkshire to Norfolk, re-structured my businesses, had a baby at 56, and got married to my beautiful wife Emily. During this period of turmoil of about three years in my personal life, which I felt was coinciding with some significant changes in my business life, I had to make some changes for the positive. I had been someone who had hated change and confronting issues that need to be dealt with. I realised that change was coming in the business world and unless I did something radical and got in front of this I could be overwhelmed and consumed by it. So I re-structured my businesses and started a new one.

What steps can you take in a crisis?

Do you panic? Do you react calmly in a crisis? The underlying solution is how do you react to these issues and problems? There have been and will be plenty of problems in your business and personal life. You need to think calmly of the underlying solution. You need to access your creative and problem solving part of your brain.

I know that when I am exhausted I shut down. When I am in full stress mode I cannot smell, or feel or think properly. Why could I not read? Too stressed. What are your sensors for: seeing, feeling, smelling, thinking? What if you lack motivation? Hit a brick wall? That happens to me for lots of reasons: I get paralysed with fear. I get very angry with myself and it spirals. Not any more. I have changed. This change takes time and I find I need to work at this every day. But the more I improve the more motivated I become.

Success and Failure:

I think success and failure are just different sides of the same coin. What I mean is that through failure I learn. Now failure is not a bad word; it is a valuable experience. I have had plenty of failures, and to name just one business I set up was "Iartbroker.com". I set this up around 2007. I had a business plan and strategy. But I did not have a "dream team". I had an idea, which was trading through the internet to sell art, a bit like ebay for art, but this failed for many reasons, some too many to list, but essentially my team was poor to not existent. I did learn, and made sure I have a great team around me going forward. A different failure was not to protect my Intellectual Property around the setting up of a business, and that is key. Not any more.

When success does come, and it will, like failure, like death, it will come. Success to me is often a brief feeling, and I want to move onto the next project. I would rather spend time with my family, go sailing, go for a walk or run and smell fresh grass or sit in the sun, rather than look at a bank balance.

7

Chapter 7: Getting personal priorities right

Whether you are conscious of it or not there will be many principles that guide you. Some of them are things you just do unconsciously, especially if you have a salaried job. But as a business owner, many of your beliefs and philosophies will be challenged, some to the core, and these are often out of your control. There are various principles I try to live by:

Family first.

This was challenged early on when my first daughter, Flavia was born whilst I was in New York for an art fair. It is an extraordinary tale, and one I was very stressed about at the time. For years I had been trying to get selected for exhibiting at a prestigious fair called "The International Fine Art Fair" in New York. As it happens I finally got "invited" in 2001 to join the 2002 edition. I had already paid my exhibition fee and was all signed up. It was looking like Flavia's expected birth date was close to when I was going to be in New York.

Fortunately, I am good at preparing and planning for events. I have always run businesses that required organisation and a great deal of advance planning. From *Master Drawings New York* and *London*, to running my own dealing business, I have had over 20 years of experience of planning ahead. This was especially tested for this fair. I had asked Anne Varick (Vara) Lauder, if she would help me on the stand in New York. Vara kindly assisted me at the fair, and was able to take over the stand during the opening night. She is someone who is incredibly knowledgeable and experienced in the art world. I had the stand all planned and all the works shipped (Fig. 18).

Fig. 18. Dr Anne Varick Lauder and author at the International Fine Art Fair, New York, circa 2002, on the author's stand

My first wife called me the night I had finished hanging all the drawings for sale in the booth[144], a process that took me hours! I remember dozing in bed with my mobile phone resting on my chest when she called saying "the baby is on the way"! I jumped into a taxi and made my way to JFK. I rushed to the

144 The preparation and display of the booth is a huge endeavor which involves a multitude of planning from choosing the wall coverings, to art works to export licenses, shipping, paperwork, payments and accomodation in the city.

first airline representative I could find and asked them when was the next flight back to London was since my wife was expecting our first child and had gone into labour. They said if I upgraded to first class, I could take Concorde[145] back to London. I said "yes". I bought the ticket and waited in the lounge. I remember thinking how crazy was this. I do not remember much of the flight since I had been up most of the last 48 hours. But I do remember the interior looking like the "Thunderbirds" movies from my childhood. One particularly cool moment was when the digital reader said we were over the Atlantic and going Mac 2.04.[146] Thankfully I got home to see Flavia, and flew back after 24 hours, just in time for the first day of the art fair.

Faith:

My Christian faith is not something I talk much about but it is central to my beliefs and actions. I feel like it has become incredibly "uncool" to mention this or to discuss this openly in British society. For some reason when people talk about faith they preface this by saying "I don't believe in God". Well I do. I guess I wanted to put this brief paragraph in since I find the teachings of Christ, and indeed many faiths, an important part of life, and I will live by this.

I need to be an optimist to be an entrepreneur. I need to believe in myself and my ambitions. Do not underestimate your value or the value of other people.

I am a late developer[147]

That is okay. There were many businessmen who were late to their success. Colonel Harland Sanders, the original Colonel C. of Kentucky Fried Chicken

---

[145] Concorde stopped flying in 2003

[146] Concorde could fly at twice the speed of sound, 1,354 miles per hour.

[147] I highly recommend a great book by Rich Karlgaard, *Late Bloomers: The Hidden Strengths of Learning and Succeeding at Your Own Pace* , 2021

recipe fame. I love his story of how at the age of 62 he would go round to restaurants with his chicken recipe franchising it. He did not accept rejection. I am okay with rejection, and as an entrepreneur or as a human being you must be okay with that and not be offended. It is often just a numbers game: someone will get your vision, as long as you persevere. You need to believe that you are extraordinary and can and will achieve great things. As an entrepreneur you must also trust your instincts. If something feels wrong do not do it. If it smells like a dog, wags its tail like a dog then it is likely to be a dog. It is easy to get pulled into rabbit holes. Early on in my career as an independent dealer, I went down a massive Alice in Wonderland type hole. I was on a buying trip to the south of France in pursuit of a drawing. I was on a train from Paris to Bezier. It was an overnight train and a French lady got me talking and said she had a collection of paintings and drawings she wanted to sell. One was by Giovanni Boldini (1842-1931) and there was a letter confirming the attribution from the artist. Anyway after I had viewed the drawings I went to go and see her and the paintings in her home. I even got them professionally photographed since this was before mobile phones and I did not have a camera with me. I did this so I could properly research them and show them to the relevant specialists on Boldini. The funny thing was that as I researched this picture and others it became clear that she had tried all the French trade, and they were all duds. I learnt to be aware of rabbit holes, there are plenty of people trying to pull you down one.

I like helping people

I started *Master Drawings London* and *Master Drawings New York* because I wanted to help colleagues. By starting an art fair focused primarily of Master Drawings I knew I could help dealers, collectors and institutions. Yes there was a commercial element to it, I would be exposing my stock and my name to more people, and this was likely to result in more sales. But I also loved the sense of collegiality created by the art fairs I founded.

The reason for starting *Art Advisory Group* was because I could help more people in the Art and Luxury Goods market, instead of just focusing on the niche area of Master Drawings. The Luxury Goods market is estimated to be US$ 471 billion and the Art Market US$ 65 billion. Surely there are some opportunities in these zones?

Doing what I say I am going to do

If I make a commitment I mean it. Whether it be to a client, colleague, family member. I mean it. My word is my bond is now rather anachronistic. Some of the more mundane but important guides for me are: be on time; polite; respectful; consistently boring is often a good thing.

Why are you doing this?

This is part of the vision, but I also feel this is worth emphasizing. Why are you creating this business? Is it because you want to make a lot of money? There are easier ways, and less risky ways to make money. Why am I putting all of my energy, and money and time into this? What is my motivator? I am going to share some of my motivations, but they are mixed, and have changed over time, and some may become more nuanced over time. We all need help, but we all need to find our own way in life. Feel the pressures and strains of earning money. It does not come easy, but it can be achieved when we apply our mind and intelligence and strength both physically and mentally. I am convinced that my goals and ambitions will be achieved.

I want to be happy?

This is a tough one. But I think it is important to do the things that make me happy. This is a complex one, and is multi-layered. I am happy doing lots of things, and this is often when I am with my children and wife, going on a walk, being outside, listening to the birds, looking at leaves and trees, sailing, being in the sunshine, walking, running. Achieving the goals that I have set myself. I wanted to set up my own business, and have set up four. I wanted to have children, and have four. I wanted to be married, and did that twice. Am I happy now? Yes. But I want more. That is human nature.

Have a vision:

The legacy of what my life is about and what I want to achieve involves charitable work, giving back to society, and helping people. I also want to build up my art collection.

Perseverance:

Keep on trying, persevere, do not give up. I know I am very determined and do not give up. Try something differently if one route does not work. Think around the problem. There is usually a solution. Ask people around you for help.

When things get tough in life, and they do, I always find it helpful to think that there is always hope. Sometimes it is difficult to see it, and you need to get the people around you to help and support you. Also things change every day: another guarantee is things do not stay the same for long. As I have said you need to understand yourself and be honest with yourself. I know I am good at looking at drawings and valuing them and giving an expert opinion of what the drawing is. I am good at organising things. I must be since I organised *Master Drawings London* for 16 years: this grew from 16 exhibiting galleries to over 40 by the time event was re-branded into *London Art Week*. I also was running *Master Drawings New York* concurrently, plus my own dealing business, all whilst living in the middle of the Yorkshire Dales, possibly the furthest point you could get from London and New York. Plus I had a young family with three children, one dog, two rabbits and two gerbils. I know I am good with paperwork, my memory for images and drawings and paintings is almost photographic. I know I am not good at computer coding, so I have a web developer, I know I am good at communicating, but for *Master Drawings New York* I knew we needed a great marketing team, so I appointed one.

As a business person you will have to learn new habits, and will have to try and be in front of the curve, rather than watching the world around you change. I have had to learn about Iphones and social media, which seem to change at the speed of light, new accounting software such as Xero, the list is endless. We are used to doing things a certain way, but we need to change and be adaptable. As a business owner you need to be able to tackle new things and not be afraid to learn.

Technology changes and inventions come at great speed. I remember when the internet and emails were first used. When I went away on my honeymoon when I first got married in 1989 I had sixteen emails after I had been away for two weeks and a pile of post and some phone messages. All of which could be dealt with on my return. Now if I do not respond to an email or a phone call within 24 hours the business has gone. Like most people I probably get sixteen emails in an hour.

I find changes remarkable and they often creep up, for example when did wheels become a thing on suit cases? I love it. What about the top of a disposable bottle being attached to the bottle, brilliant. Change happens quickly and your inventions will be copied and adapted by other people. Think of fast food restaurants. The revolutionary checkouts adopted by McDonalds and used by Subway or Leon.

Now AI is here and I feel it is like the internet all over again, but on steroids. There seems to be a rush towards it and we all do not know where it is taking us. I want to understand what is going on and be part of that journey. I used the new tool on Google of uploading photos and finding it on the web. A fantastic new resource. I was able to find the drawing I was researching within seconds. Amazing.

Change in the auction world. Change in the way business is done.

Over the 37 years in the Art Market I have seen the dominance of the Christie's and Sotheby's duopoly change. There are now more specialist auction houses in the UK, and in the world, both in physical premises, and on-line. That is all very exciting to see how this changes and develops.

Dealers often live in a silo, it is them against their world and the world against them, a bit like farmers. That is not necessarily a bad thing, and indeed they need to focus on what they do, and do that very well.

Experience is crucial; it does not matter how many initials are after you name; have you been exposed to this or that type of situation?

I did see working remotely as the way to go as a dealer and did not have the gallery overheads. This was something I have been doing since 1998. This did mean my overheads could be kept down. However I did have to attend a lot of art fairs and pop up events. I was also someone who was not very good at sitting still, and the thought of staying put for months in a gallery filled me with horror.

What is the measurement of success?

Success can mean more money; it can mean survival. Success is qualified in many different ways, depending on who you are. This is why I ask what do you want to achieve, what does fulfilling those successes look like? On my death bed do I want to say, wow I love looking at my bank balance? No, I want to be with the people I love and who care about me, and look down the end of that long path with the knowledge I did my bit to make this world a better place.

8

Chapter 8: Some of the Great Collectors and Dealers I have met

Some people might be surprised that I am putting collectors and dealers together. But it is my view that great dealers and collectors often think in the same way. Collectors like to buy, and sell their objects sometimes, and dealers like to buy, and sometimes keep their best buys, or indeed the ones they cannot sell, in their private collection. I worked with Robert Kashey[148] who was always incredibly generous with his knowledge and sold him drawings that I was exhibiting in New York. He had a fabulous perspective and empathy towards objects, especially his passion for 19th century sculpture. Dino Tomasso[149] was someone I knew of for a long time, and then when I moved to the Yorkshire Dales, coincidentally he moved to the next village, we became firm friends. His attitude to buying was "I like it and I will have it". David Lachemann[150] is an extraordinary dealer and collector and buys the most exquisite drawings. In New York the twin brothers Paul and John Herring were extremely generous in showing their fabulous collection of drawings. Some had been bought from

---

[148] Robert Kashey has had a gallery in New York, Shepherd Gallery, since 1966.

[149] Dino Tomasso has a gallery in Leeds and London.

[150] David Lachemann is a dealer who works privately, which means he does not have a gallery space.

the Chatsworth sales and were just wonderful to see in person, since this was before I had started to work in the market.

Earl Gowrie and Francis Bacon

When I was working at Sotheby's one of the early invitations we had as graduate trainees was a drinks party to meet Grey Gowrie at his flat in London. He was Chairman of Sotheby's Europe from 1987-1994. I remember meeting him, with the other graduate trainees, and the first thing that struck like a bolt of lightening was the huge Francis Bacon painting in his sitting room. He was charming, and felt very lucky to have met him.

Through the years when I was working at all four major auction houses I met many of the great collectors and art dealers, either indirectly or directly and it was fascinating to see them. At Phillips I met the amazing German collector Dr Wolfgang Ratjen[151]. At Sotheby's, I met Sam and Paul Josefowitz.[152] I first met George Abrams[153] at Phillips and his late wife Maida. I have seen some amazing art collections.

I got to see the beautiful collection of British and European oil sketches from the 18th and 19th centuries belonging to the late John and Charlotte Gere [154] in their home in London, before it was donated to the National Gallery, London, on long-term loan.

De Ganay

[151] Dr Wolfgang Ratjen (1944-1997) was a collector of German and Italian Old Master Prints and Drawings, and a philanthropist.

[152] Sam Josefowitz (1921-2015) collected French late nineteenth-century paintings and prints, especially of the Pont-Aven school, and prints by Rembrandt. His son Paul Josefowitz (1952-2010) was a collector and owned the Apollo magazine from 1992-2002.

[153] George and Maida Abrams had an amazing collection of Dutch and Flemish drawings from the 16th and 17th Centuries. It has been largely donated to the Harvard museums in Boston.

[154] John Gere (1921-1995) was a Keeper at the British Museum and Charlotte Gere (b.1937) is an art historian and author.

One of my closest friends from university is Oliver Sarkozy, and still is today. We became close friends for many reasons, and I was drawn to him because of his sense of fun and adventure and love of music. His family connections were rooted in France, and his mother was a de Ganay. One holiday he invited me to come over and stay in Paris with his grandparents, it happened to be close in time to my application to Sotheby's graduate trainee programme, which will become relevant later. His mother's family own an amazing house called Château de Corance (Fig. 19.1-4) and I was invited to a lunch with the family, and got to see their amazing art collection. I did not realise at the time that Sotheby's were preparing an important sale of their collection in Monaco (Fig. 19.4). I was fortunate enough to see many of the paintings and drawings in situ, and works by Francesco Guardi and Leonardo da Vinci -yes the grisaille paintings or oil sketches. What I remember most vividly was calling the grande dame "tu" not "vous", which did not go down well.

Coincidentally a few months later I was being interviewed by the Chairman of Sotheby's, Graham Llewellyn, who said in passing that he saw my name in the visitor's book at the Château.

Fig. 19.1 Author outside Château de Corance

Fig. 19.2 Oliver Sarkozy at Fontainebleau

Fig. 19.3 Château de Corance

Fig. 19.4 Sotheby's auction catalogue of the de Ganay collection in Monaco in 1989

Professor Ray Pahl

I first met Ray-Professor Raymond Pahl, FBA (1935-2011)- when I was working at Phillips. He had already been buying for many years and was a sophisticated buyer of Old Master Drawings and Modern British Art. He was one of the rare breed left of academic buyers. By that I mean he was a university academic who bought for the thrill of the chase, and I had many exciting discussions with him. When Ray sadly died he entrusted to me to sell his large collection of prints, drawings and paintings, which I did over a number of years.

Sir Brinsley Ford:

Another amazing private collector I got to meet and whose collection I got to was Sir Brinsley Ford (1908-1999). He was a collector, art historian and museum donor. Sir Brinsley Ford was an incredible man. Shortly after leaving Oxford University he had the opportunity to buy a great drawing by Michelangelo. This came up for auction at the famous Henry Oppenheimer sale at Christie's. He bought the drawing for 3,400 guineas in 1936. This drawing was subsequently sold by his executors for £8,143,750 (including premium) in 2000. He is quoted as being reprimanded by one of his relatives for spending such a considerable amount of money on an artwork, at the time about the equivalent cost of a house. I was lucky to see his private collection whilst he was still alive, and he very generously showed the Michelangelo together with his extraordinary collection of six *Punchinello Drawings* by Giandomenico Tiepolo (1727-1804). These were also sold at Christie's, on 3 December 2019, for a combined total of £3,871,500. He was charming and shared his knowledge and enthusiasm for the beautiful objects he owned. He donated his book archive to the Paul Mellon Centre for studies in British Art, and 55 art works have been gifted by Sir Brinsley's son to the National Trust property at Osterley Park, where they are on permanent view.

Other great collectors I have met are dealer turned collector Jeffrey Horvitz. I have mentioned him earlier when I sold him a drawing by Baccio Bandinelli when I first started dealing. He and his wife Carol have recently donated their collection of French 16th-19th century Art to The Art Institute of Chicago. It consists of a massive collection of 2,000 drawings, 500 paintings and 50 sculptures. Included amongst his collection are some works I sold to him.

I never met Eugene Victor Thaw (1927-2018), but he is a well known author on the American drip painter Jackson Pollock and contributed to the definitive catalogue on the artist. His collecting and dealing field was extensive and his influence amongst collectors and dealers is well known and often talked about. The Morgan Library & Museum and Metropolitan Museum, both in New York, received significant donations of drawings and works of art from his collection. In his later life he collected native American art work when he and his wife retired to New Mexico, and these were donated to Fenimore Art Museum, New York.

A dealer turned collector I would have liked to have met would have been Frits Lugt. His extraordinary work ethic and ability to put order and category in the field of collecting is primarily known to me through his two volumes on collectors' marks[155], which is the standard reference work for any collector or dealer in works on paper. Reading his biography is an eye opening experience to someone who worked in this field for decades. His dedication to the education and dissemination of information was unwavering. The number of books he published is extraordinary. The Foundation he and his wife, Jacoba Klever, created in Paris in 1947 -Fondation Custodia- Collection Frits Lugt must be seen to be believed. The collection is located in the Hôtel Turgot, and in addition to the extensive collection of drawings has rare books, portrait miniatures, paintings, antiquities, stained glass, antique frames, sculptures, furniture and Chinese porcelain.

---

[155] *Les Marques de collections de dessins & d'estampes*, published in 1921, and the *Supplément* of 1956, and is constantly updated on-line by the Foundation.

Sir Harold Acton

When I was working in Florence at Sotheby's in 1986, I got invited to see Sir Harold Acton's[156] villa and art collection just outside Florence at Villa Pietra. A friend of my father, the late Billa Harrod[157], knew Sir Harold, and kindly wrote to him to introduce me. So when I was in Florence I called the villa and was instructed to take a bus outside Florence, and the bus would stop opposite the entrance to the villa. All indeed happened as the butler had said, but he did not mention that the gates would lead onto a Cyprus drive which seemed to stretch about ½ a mile. Standing at the entrance was a butler in a white liveried jacket. As I walked down the drive, which seemed to take a long time, I took in the smells of the wonderful trees, all sweet and smelling of that distinct Italian and Mediterranean feel of hot summers.

The butler handed me the largest gin and tonic I had ever tasted, and seemed mostly gin with a splash of tonic.

As I walked through the incredible Villa I was struck by how amazing the whole house seemed and Sir Harold was a kindly gentleman. He made some small talk and asked me what exhibitions I had seen recently and I mentioned that I had seen a recent exhibition on Donatello[158] and his circle, and he mentioned in an off hand, not a showy off way, oh I think I leant four pieces to that exhibition.

I had heard that the Italian garden was something that was especially beautiful at the villa and he kindly took me on a tour of the garden, with the most incredible views over the city (Fig. 20.4), which sadly can not be seen from my rather poor 1980s photo.

---

[156] Sir Harold Acton (1904-1994) was a British scholar and writer and aesthete.

[157] Wilhelmine Margaret Eve, Lady Harrod (1911 –2005), known as Billa Harrod, was a writer and architectural conservationist, and the wife of the economist Sir Roy Harrod.

[158] Donatello (c.1386-1466) is a Florentine sculptor who is considered one of the greatest sculptors of all time.

Fig. 20.1 Author in the garden of the Peggy Guggenheim Museum, 1987, with Hans Arp's sculpture behind, "Amphora"

Fig. 20.2 Author on the Grand Canal, Venice, during a regatta

Fig. 20.3 Sir Harold Acton in his Garden at Villa "La Pietra", 1986, on author's visit

Fig. 20.4 The Italianate garden, at Villa "La Pietra", Florence, on author's visit

When I was working in Venice I was introduced to Paolo Barozzi[159] who was one of the last links to when Peggy Guggenheim was living in her Palazzo dei Leoni, on the Grand Canal, now the museum which houses all of her collection. I worked there as an intern for two months in the summer of 1987. I had managed to secure one of the sought after places as an intern at the museum. Paolo was her private secretary and assistant. We had a lot of fun going out in Venice with him, and here is a photo of him and John Martin (Fig. 21).

Fig. 21, Paolo Barozzi and John Martin, Venice, 1987.

[159] Paolo Barozzi, *Peggy Guggenheim, Una donna, una collezione, Venezia*, 1982

9

Chapter 9: Art As an Investment:

No art book writing about the Art Market would be complete unless I include something about Art as an Investment. Firstly most people buy an object, any artwork, whether it be a painting, drawing, sculpture, or luxury good because it is a "passion purchase". This is complex because it covers emotions and money. The latter is easier to quantify, not the former. When I buy any object, as a dealer, or now as a collector, I buy it because I like it. More than that, I buy it because there is an emotional connection, a spark, between me and the object. Also I buy it because I can afford it. When I bought as a dealer I purchased the art work because I thought I could make money from the object, and usually did. That is difficult to quantify, and to verbalise, but as I said earlier I know what I like when I see it. Everyone approaches buying artwork differently, and everyone brings their own reasons, emotions and experiences. That is one of the reasons why prices can be pushed up at auction since people attach different values to the same object. The same object is valued differently by different people.

For example when the most expensive painting was sold at auction, Leonardo da Vinci's *Salvator Mundi*, [160] the pre-sale estimate was around US $100 million. This was thought, amongst the trade, to be too high. But we were wrong. It

[160] Christie's New York, 15 November 2017, sold for $450,312,500

sold for US $450 million. And this is the most expensive painting sold at auction ever. For now. There are many stories around this painting, and the history around this extraordinary picture is fascinating and well documented. I was one of the 30,000 people who got to see it in New York on exhibition in 2017. Many things went right for the vendor and Christie's. It was sold by the family trust of Dmitry Rybolovlev, a Russian billionaire, and was bought by Abu Dhabi's Department of Culture and Tourism for the Louvre Abu Dhabi. I think this is a brilliant purchase for many reasons, and will continue to intrigue the public and experts for many years to come. I for one want to see it again in Abu Dhabi.

Would this painting sell for same amount the following day or 6 months on? Would it sell for more or less if it was to come back on the market? This is all academic, but the point I am making is that the price achieved on the day is the market price for this art work, at this moment in time. We know the same painting sold at another public auction just twelve years earlier, in 2005, also in the USA, for just US $10,000. The reasons for this painting selling for 1/2 billion are complex, but involve: market context, research, marketing, market opinion and other forces. This can be applied to any object, but of course most objects are not like this one.

Understanding how the market works:

Why did the same artwork sell for such as huge discrepancy? This is a good example of how the art frictions, and unknowns, which are baked into the objects and the market affect the value of an art work. This also illustrates how people make money in the Art Market, from dealers to collectors. The final, almost perfect context for the sale of the *Salvator Mundi*, illustrates a number of factors of how the market works. I think it is worth going through these to show how these different factors affect the value of the object.

The first is attribution. Without going into the weeds too much, the general consensus is this painting was sold in 2005 as a copy after Leonardo, whilst in 2017 it was sold as an original work by the artist. This change in attribution can and does have a significant affect to the values of an object, and the same principal can be applied to any category whether it be a wine, car, ceramic or a pair of sneakers. This is where expertise comes in and I believe is one of the fundamentals of the market. When you buy an object you need to know what you are buying. This is where my experience of over 30 years kicks in.

The second is provenance or history of the object. It is important to understand that unless you are buying an object directly from the artist any object has a complex history. I find it wonderfully mind blowing to think about how many people have owned an object. Most of this history will be lost. Some of this information will be retained by the current owner, but most of it will be lost. I have seen this time and again during my working career in the Art Market. Many of the objects I have handled are hundreds of years old and the known history is often brief to non existent. This is one of the factors baked into the market. There are a number of red flags to watch out for in the history of any object. These are often the most obvious, such as how has the object come on the market? By that I mean who is offering you the object to buy. You must ask questions around the ownership. Since there is no register of objects, such as the Land Registry in the UK for land and property, you must satisfy yourself the owner is the genuine owner. What is the known history and what proof do they have? This can come in the form of public auctions, what are the details of this? Can you look them up or can the owner show you these details. Often you will find further provenance mentioned in these catalogues. If the object is of significance it may be published in a catalogue raisonné or exhibition catalogue. You need to see the exact details of this, what is exactly written about the object. In relation to the *Salvator Mundi* this painting had recently been accepted as by Leonardo by all the relevant experts on the artist, and was included in the recent exhibition in London[161].

The third factor is the object itself. What does it look like. Is it beautiful? How big it is it? What is the wall power of the object? These are all very subjective factors that have a significant affect on its value. Simple things like a figure in the picture increases the value over no figures. I have found

---

[161] London, The National Gallery, *Leonardo da Vinci: Painter at the Court of Milan*, 9 November 2011-5 February 2012, no. 91.

that depictions of anatomy and seascapes are more popular that studies of a landscapes with trees and no figures. These nuances do affect the value. This can be applied to any objects, such as cars or luxury goods. Going back to the Leonardo it was generally felt that the striking image of Christ had a wow factor that had to be experienced. When I saw the painting on exhibition in New York it was an incredibly moving experience. The image has incredible wall power.

The fourth factor is the condition of the object. This is something that is also very subjective, and the nuances are often known and understood by conservators and market specialists. If you are buying a table or any piece of furniture you need to understand which parts may be restored. The same goes for paintings or cars. Market professionals will know what to look for and expect. It is my experience that an object gets bashed and dropped frequently, and I can expect any object to have been handled and dropped a lot. In relation to the *Salvator Mundi* the same applies, it is over 500 years old and will have had some re-painting.

The fifth factor is around the marketing of the object, market forces and context. This is where the magic happens. By that I mean the magic for the seller. If you present an important object at auction in the right conditions this will spark interest to a wider public. This happens around single owner sales, such as the sale of the contents of an important country house that have been owned by the family for generations[162], or the sale of the jewels belonging the Duchess of Windsor[163], or dresses belonging to Princess Diana[164] or the studio sale from Damien Hirst.[165] This is a complex mix of market buzz and hype and it is the work of the auction house to generate as much interest as possible. Sometimes the object is so important it is best not sold at auction

[162] *The Attic Sale*, Holkham Hall, 11 February, 2025 held by Sworders, with 97% sold.

[163] The auction was at Sotheby's Geneva in 1987, 2- 3 April, and the collection sold for US $53.5 million.

[164] Christie's New York, 25 June, 1997, raised US $ 3.25 for her charities.

[165] 15 and 16 September 2008, Sotheby's London, "Beautiful Inside my Head Forever" auction sold for £111 million.

and the work is presented behind closed doors but the deal is done with the involvement of trustees and agents. This is how many of the important works of art are bought by institutions and museums. I know because I have been lucky to have been part of these transactions.

Regulation in the Art Market:

Firstly I should say something about the Art Market being unregulated in the UK. By that I mean it is not regulated by the Financial Conduct Authority (FCA), in the same way that other industries such as pensions, financial investments, insurance, banking, motor vehicle purchases, credit cards and cryptoassets are regulated. There are many consumer laws I must follow as a business. There are however, plenty of rules and regulations around the export and import of cultural goods. There are plenty of regulations around the description of selling an object. There are plenty of rules around receiving money and around employment.

The Anti Money Laundering (AML) directive came into effect on 10 January 2020. In the UK all Art Market participants must follow these rules and regulations. What this has meant, apart from all the registration and courses that need to be followed by businesses, is that all financial transactions over 10,000 Euros need to put through the AML system. There is a lot of detail I will not discuss here but one of the net effects has been that buyers have been put off from trading with UK participants. Many of the buyers just go somewhere else, where the directive has not yet come into effect. This is a good thing if that buyer was transacting in a fraudulent way, but there are also many buyers who merely wish to remain anonymous and have found other routes to their purchases, such as in the USA, where currently there are no AML laws. However on 23 July 2025 the Art Market Integrity Act was introduced to the Senate, and this will require US Art Market businesses to follow similar regulations to the UK, and European Art Markets.

I am in favour of making any changes to the Art Market which increases buyers and sellers confidence in the market. Security measures to prevent fraud around the transaction process are important to get right.

Trading regulations can change depending on the sentiment of governments and public opinion. This change can happen at short notice and have a significant impact on the Art Market and trading in these markets. Often these are highly emotive subjects. One example was the ivory ban in the UK, which came into effect on 2 June 2022. The effect on the antiques market has been disastrous. It is my view that there were perfectly good laws in place already, and this was replaced by a total ban on antique ivory. There are many instances when ivory was included in antique furniture, from pianos to violins, to miniatures and haircombs. None of these can be bought or sold, now with very few exceptions. I completely abhor the trading of modern ivory and animal horns and skins. I will not go into the weeds on this very toxic topic, which is a bit like Brexit in that the opposing sides became very entrenched.

The other significant recent change in trading regulations was a new import licensing regulation[166], which came into effect in June 2025. This is incredibly complex and the effect is still playing out, but it has sent sigificant shock waves through the antiques market.

Both of these laws have come from a place of wanting to do something good, one to achieve a total ban in the trading of ivory, and the other to stop the trade in illicit antiques. These are very complex areas and it is my view governing bodies do not have the time, energy or willingness to listen properly to the market, for whatever reasons.

Friction in the market:

There are many barriers and frictions in the Art Market, which have the net effect of making this a relatively small market financially, and I have gone

---

[166] Regulation (EU 2019/880).

into these figures in the preface to this book. Indeed the whole of the global Art Market trades under what one global company trades. The international courier company, FedEx, has a turnover larger than the global Art Market. The turnover of FedEx in 2023 was over US$ 90 billion, whilst the Art Market was around US$ 65 billion for a similar period. Thank you to Gregory Rook, for giving me that figure. Gregory is a specialist in Contemporary Art.

Purchases in the Art Market can cost a few pounds to significant amounts of money. It is not unreasonable to ask "will my money retain its value" or even "will it increase in value" or "my ambition is to make money, is this possible"? All of these are relevant questions, but there is no guarantee. Some buyers, the speculative buyers or the investment buyers are quick to follow new trends from NFTs, to digital art or whatever the next hot area of the market may be. Investors are often the elephant in the room and are regarded by some sectors as being vulgar or somehow not worthy of the art. My view is firmly there is a financial transaction going on and whether someone makes money or not is irrelevant. There is a buyer and seller. The reality is many people are coming into the market as investors, and whether this is positive or negative or just how people perceive the asset class that is where we are. I see this as growing significantly as the transparency in the market grows, the frictions get ironed out, as well as knowledge of the market and how it works.

I find the role as an art adviser is to explain the different complexities of the market and to assist our clients to make informed decisions and awareness of the opportunities in the market. That opinion is based on my experience and expertise from 37 years in the market, plus I am drawing on expertise and experience of my team of art experts, many of whom have decades of experience in the Art Market, like myself. Currently I work with a team of over 90 contracted specialists, and I see this growing to 200-300 in the next 2-3 years.

Due diligence:

As a dealer and now as an art advisor and Art Market professional, I know how to go about research. This is not just checking that the object is what it says it is, but involves doing a deep dive into the object's history, and knowing where the pitfalls exist. Often these objects are hundreds or thousands of years old and it is just not possible to fill in many of the gaps. My team and I are well versed in the pitfalls and know where to look for red flags, and what the red flags are. The problems occur for buyers and sellers when they ignore many of the standard and often quite easy checks that can made by an Art Market researcher. The due diligence done by the buyer can vary enormously and is influenced by how curious and questioning the buyer is, how much of the market do they know, what are the market traditions? The seller is morally obliged to reveal all the known provenance, but unless they sign a contract to that effect how much do they reveal? Sometimes this information is suppressed for normal commercial reasons, sometimes for confidentiality.

Liquidity in the market

The nature of the Art Market means that many of the objects being sold are not liquid. It is regarded as an illiquid market. In comparison, selling a stock or share is a simple process. The trade can be done in minutes. In selling art and second hand luxury goods, the process is more complex, and there are may variables. Each asset class can have a different platform to sell. Broadly speaking there is either auction or private sale. Each of these routes has many twists and turns, and it requires experience and knowledge to know what route to take. It is not as simple as I will take my object to the nearest auction house or dealer and I will get the market price. The painting that I describe in the second paragraph of this chapter illustrates that. This is how dealers and collectors make money, because a person wants to sell, it appears at auction, and they buy it. It is what I did for 25 years.

There other many other asset classes from collectibles such as Toys, magazines, Cars and Motor vehicles, all have their own and unique risks and opportunities. The opportunities exist in any of these markets. You have to be prepared to put in the time, effort, money and energy to become an expert in any of these fields, or at least the person who knows the most about a particular collecting field. As I have detailed in this book, I obsessed in just one small field, the Old Master Drawings market.

Fractionalisation

To try and address some of the illiquidity in the market, various tools have been created to try and make this illiquid asset more liquid. One tool is fractionalisation. I can see this being applied more to those areas of the market where there are simply investing for these reasons, and do not want to be a single owner. Fractionalisation is essentially turning an object into a stock and splitting it up into pieces and selling. A bit like people buying into shares in a horse, "halvsies" gone crazy, ot split into 100 or 1,000 shares. This is usually reserved for works of art worth above say £1,000,000. Now this has appeal to many people who would not traditionally buy works of art, so some people love to say is making the art world "democratic". Frankly I do not buy this argument. It is a financial instrument, which is fine. But do not pretend it is making the art world less elitist. What is wrong with excellence, expertise, quality, ability, and yes this is by its nature elitist? Just recently it was announced that the owner of the Leiden collection, Thomas S. Kaplan, the billionaire investor, was in advanced plans to fractionalise the collection on the US stock exchange. The Leiden collection is an incredible collection of Dutch "Golden Age" paintings, and is the only private collection to own sixteen paintings by Rembrandt, and the only Vermeer painting in private hands. It will be interesting to see how this develops.

Digital art

The market in Digital art and NFT's [Non-Fungible Token] is still in its infancy, and has seen some significant ups and downs in the last few years. Digital art is an artistic work that uses digital technology as part of the creative process. This was brought into the spot light when Christie's in New York, sold on 11

March 2021, a work by Mike Winkelmann under the alias Beeple, an NFT, *Every days: the First 5,000 Days* for $69,346,250.

What are the measurables?

There are numerous on-line indices used to track the value of items sold at auction. For fine art, such as paintings, drawings, prints and sculptures there is Art Sales Index, Artnet, Invaluable, and as a general overview of the market the Sotheby's Mei Moses index, which tracks sectors of the market. These are helpful tools in seeing what sold at auction, but the nuances of what was the condition of the work, what was the market sentiment like at the auction, the wider economy do not get reflected through the simple figures given from the auction. This is where market knowledge comes in, and helps to decipher these results.

The private market of selling through a dealer to a collector or another dealer or institution or collector to collector is by its nature private and unknown. This is where the market gets its most criticism for being opaque. I am not here to defend that type of transaction, but just explain how it works. I do not think this will significantly change since this transaction is private, and why should this be public knowledge?

Art and money will always be tied to together, and this is a just a factor of human nature, and the value we assign to each is also deeply personal and subjective.

What are the opportunities:

I do believe that there are many opportunities to buy in the Art Market, and make finds and discoveries which can be both incredibly satisfying and profitable. The joy of owning a beautiful drawing, painting, sculpture or object is endless. I find looking at the objects I own, now as a collector, incredibly satisfying and life enhancing.

Index

Endorsements

Reader Reviews

"Both entertaining and informative, Crispian's book offers a valuable and comprehensive insight into the art market."

Andrew McKenzie, specialist in Old Masters and author on Scottish history, most recently *Scotland's Nostradamus, A Quest for the Brahan Seer.*

"Crispian Riley-Smith's account of the art world over the last 35 plus years is a fascinating and packed full of advice for anyone wishing to build their careers today."

Cheyenne Westphal, independent art dealer and advisor.

About the Author

An entrepreneur from childhood, Crispian is a respected art expert in Old Master Drawings. After St. Andrews University, where he gained an MA in Art History, he has worked in the four largest auction houses in London. This is his first book, however he has written articles in the following magazines and academic journals including *Apollo, County Life, Antique Collecting, Master Drawings, Galleries Magazine*, and countless entries in his catalogues as a dealer. He has lectured for the *York Georgian Society* and *Kirker Holidays*. He also founded and ran *Crispian Riley-Smith Fine Arts Ltd*, which he still owns and runs, *Master Drawings London*, *Master Drawings New York*, and now *Art Advisory Group Ltd.*

His first book is part memoir, and part self-help for other entrepreneurs, investors in the Art Market, students and the curious. Crispian lives in Norfolk with his family.

You can connect with me on:

- https://artadvisorygroupltd.com
- https://www.linkedin.com/in/crispian-riley-smith

Subscribe to my newsletter:

✉ https://www.linkedin.com/newsletters/newsletter-7332350520461848577

Printed in Dunstable, United Kingdom

72893561R00080